ORIGINAL KNITTING
SANDY BLACK

ORIGINAL KNITTING
SANDY BLACK

UNWIN HYMAN

London Sydney

First published in Great Britain by Unwin
Hyman, an imprint of Unwin Hyman Limited,
1987

UNWIN HYMAN LIMITED
Denmark House, 37–39 Queen Elizabeth Street,
London SE1 2QB
and
40 Museum Street, London WC1A 1LU

Allen & Unwin Australia Pty Ltd
8 Napier Street, North Sydney, NSW 2060,
Australia

Allen & Unwin New Zealand Ltd with the Port
Nicholson Press
60 Cambridge Terrace, Wellington, New Zealand

ISBN 0 04 440053 5

Cataloguing in Publication data

Black, Sandy
  Sand Black original knitting.
  1. Knitting——Patterns
  I. Title
  746.43′2041   TT820

Designed by **The Unknown**
Typeset by MS Filmsetting Limited, Frome,
Somerset
Printed in Italy by Motta, Milan.

ACKNOWLEDGEMENTS

Photography: Photographs of all modelled
garments by David McIntyre **except** Iris
cardigan pictures which are by Barbara
Bellingham. **Close-up photographs:** Paul
Dennison and Barbara Bellingham. **Hair:** Ian
at Power Cuts, Brighton; Ellie Wakamatsu.
Make-up: Becky Tear; Ellie Wakamatsu.
Styling: Helen Carey. **Cover Photograph:**
David McIntyre; hair and make-up Ellie
Wakamatsu; dress by Juliet Poyser; model
Pallas. **Cover close-up: Paul Dennison.**
Jacket flap portrait: Roger Riley.
I am grateful to the following companies for
lending items for photography: **Clothes:**
Juliet Poyser, Fenwicks, Bymail, Warehouse,
Ally Capellino, Maxfield Parrish, Stephanie
Cooper, Inwear, Qui, Matinique, Lek,
Foundation III. **Jewellery:** Adrian Mann,
Catylyst, Kim Ellwood. **Shoes:** Warehouse,
Office Shoes, Dolcis. **Hats:** Sandra Phillips.
Cloves and Scarves: Cornelia James.
I would like to thank Tessa Dennison for her
enthusiastic assistance with the patterns and
Frances Kennett for her invaluable help.
Thanks are also due to Anita Shuetz and
Marilyn Wilson for pattern checking; Rowan
Yarns for supplying yarns; models Tatiana,
Pallas, Carolyn and Simon at Z, Anna-
Veronica, Elliot, Julie and Virge at Look,
Isobel at Unique; and not forgetting Ted the
Fish and Elana for their impromptu
modelling!
Special thanks to the knitters and finishers:
Elaine Clarke, Audrey Day, Mary Dent, Mrs
Fisher, Lesley Fussell, Mrs Ellis, Lorainne
Hackett, Gwen King, Rene Koster, Mrs Lane,
Mrs Marshall, Mrs Oliver, Ellen Purslow,
Maureen Taylor, Pat Turner, June Wheeler,
Pauline Williams, and those whose names I
don't know — all greatly appreciated.

CONTENTS

INTRODUCTION

Fashion buyers talk of a designer having a certain 'handwriting' by which they identify their work. I have often thought that I have several different 'signatures', as many people know me for completely different syles of knitting!

This collection of patterns illustrates the extensive range of ideas and styles throughout my work and includes many of my own particular favourites.

I have always worked on a great variety of ideas at any one time, so I have grouped the designs themselves under four main headings: Graphic, Floral, Heraldic and Ornamental, each of which contains a wide selection of patterns within the main theme. Each theme has unique lasting qualities and can be traced through my work like a thread linking the past to the present.

The Graphic section demonstrates variety and fun with colour using mainly stocking stitch for designs based on simple lines and curves. It also includes knits on the linear theme which are simple but stylish modern classics.

In the Ornamental section, there are more intricately patterned and textured designs in rich colourings, inspired by all forms of decorative arts, from ceramic tiles to stained glass windows. Patterns from these sources have then been interpreted to make eyecatching designs.

The designs in the Heraldic section contain elements of the ideas from both the Graphic and Ornamental themes: the garments contain strong graphic imagery in rich bold colours combined to create highly ornamental effects.

No-one should ever tire of Floral imagery – graceful lines and pretty colourings can be endlessly restyled to look fresh. I have used flowers to decorate simple sweaters and glamorous evening wear.

The book is for anyone and everyone who enjoys knitting – whether a beginner or a more competent knitter. Both will find plenty of inspiration and scope to extend their horizons.

I have written the book for an average knitter who knows how to cast on and off, knit in stocking stitch and rib, and work simple increasings and decreasings. For the absolute beginner, there are many good reference books to teach these skills.

Every pattern is written in careful detail with step by step explanations of each technique and hints on achieving the best results. In addition, there are suggestions on how to

vary the designs by using different colours, yarn or sizing. As a further source of ideas I have described my approach to the main elements of the design process.

The garments themselves range from casual sweaters and cardigans for everyday wear, to sumptuous coats and jackets for special occasions. Some designs look equally good on men and women, and several adaptations and designs are included especially for men.

The designs are not graded in degree of difficulty, as knitters' skills vary greatly. However, there is an explanation at the beginning of each pattern which describes the techniques and methods used, from which you can make your own assessment of whether or not you can achieve the end result. Some designs in the book are fairly complex to knit, but others are deceptively easy! Everyone will find something within their capabilities, and having made one successful garment, will gain the confidence to move on to the next one.

When you have knitted several designs, and absorbed the explanations of technique given throughout the book, you may feel confident enough to try out your own simple variations such as transposing one pattern into another shaped garment, or changing the yarn used for a particular design, or even designing something new, without the results being disastrous! I hope many readers will move on to this stage, for then I will have succeeded in one of the most important aims for my book. Although I learnt to knit as a child, it was whilst at university (studying maths) that my interest in knitting really developed, and I started to design and make knitted clothes. This unusual beginning had its advantages in that, being self-taught, I was not restricted in any way by other people's ideas. Once I had learnt the basics of knitting, there was nothing to prevent me taking it as far as I wanted to, as I knew of no boundaries to what could or could not be done. I felt I could translate almost any idea into knitting – it was purely a matter of working out a logical way of doing it. This approach clearly owed something to my maths background and for me there was a natural relationship between the two areas. One result of this was that I put many ideas and techniques together in each piece of work, creating complex designs. I had little idea of their relative complexity until I had to train other people to knit them for me! I soon became more selective and refined many of my ideas, but I still enjoy creating the really complicated designs.

The natural environment and landscape was a particularly strong theme for some time, starting off very literally with pictorial sweaters and cushions, and extending into more abstract use of the patterns to be found in land and sky. I would spend much time in ensuring that I had just the right combinations of colour and texture to

achieve the effects I wanted – angora for fluffy clouds, chenille for dense bushes, bouclé yarns for trees and shiny rayon for watery effects. It was so exciting to discover a yarn buried in a mass of oddments which was exactly what I needed to complete a picture. This early exploration with yarn and texture continues in that I still take great care to match the image and the materials and still find the same excitement in doing so. Today of course there are hosts of colours and new yarns becoming available all the time, and I know I shall never stop knitting whilst I can still be inspired by a ball of yarn! By combining yarns from several different sources to achieve the effects I want, I can create a completely individual look, and this book gives details of how you can do so too. The yarns I prefer to work with always have some surface or textural interest, for example, hairy effects such as mohair and angora, the velvet of chenille, or the unevenness of bumpy 'gimped' yarn, such as the wool and cotton I have used throughout the book. I find these yarns particularly successful, because the texture of each one is interesting without overpowering the design possibilities or obliterating the structures of the knitting.

The greatest attraction of knitting is the fact that a fabric is created from nothing but a length of yarn. Everything is within the knitter's own control – the fibre, the quality, handle and weight. It can be a fine or heavy piece, knitted loosely or tight in an infinite variety of stitches and constructions which are limited only by the knitter's imagination. I have always been very attracted by colour, especially combinations of solid colour and irregular patternings and shapes, and so I have specialised a great deal in 'intarsia' knitting by hand and machine. This is a very versatile method of knitting where as many colours as desired can be used in a single row to create any image or pattern. The starting point of this sort of designing is the drawing out of the image or pattern, which is then translated to graph form.

I particularly like my designs to be non-repetitive, and sometimes treat the body rather like a blank canvas to be covered with shapes and graphic images, combined with interesting textures. Often the images break out of the two-dimensional flat surface and extend into three-dimensional reality. In other designs I ignore seam lines and continue the patterns over the whole garment, carefully matching the image at the seams to create a total effect. Examples of all these ideas can be found in the following pages.

My natural inclination is to work on a great variety of different themes at the same time – some soft and pretty flower designs, and some bright, brash and geometric, for example. I prefer a collection of designs to contain several ideas rather than too many variations on one theme. It seems that one idea bounces off or reacts with another to produce fresh thoughts in each area. I can then return to expand any one idea by creating changes of style, yarn and colour, or perhaps just taking certain elements of one pattern and working with those to produce new designs.

I have tried to convey something of this process throughout the book – to encourage the reader to look around the central ideas as they appear. The simplest way to give a design a new look is to change the colours. Follow the guidelines given and you will soon develop the careful eye needed to invent colourways of your own choice.

Sometimes a design idea is developed on the needles, on other occasions it arises from the excitement of flat pattern on paper. However the design process comes about, the important element is the central idea or theme which sparks the whole sequence off. I gather my inspiration from everywhere – from my surroundings, from travel, exhibitions, books, visits to museums and so on. An idea may spring from a tiny detail found in the decoration of a shop front, from the myriad patterns of a fairground or the graceful lines and colours of a flower. In short, anything which I find visually exciting and stimulating can be my starting point. There are no hard and fast rules. I observe wherever I go, and note down anything of interest, make little sketches, take photographs, and so on. If you follow this method, you will gradually build up a valuable store-house of possible ideas to develop. A scrap-book of postcards, picture cuttings, pieces of fabric, dried flowers and anything you find attractive is just as valuable for reference.

When I have established my initial idea, the next stage is to find the best yarn or combination of yarns in which to work. This is the start of the sampling process which is a means of investigating all the different possibilities. For a designer, this stage can never be missed out or skimped on – the successful design is always the result of many preliminary samples, each one varying one aspect such as stitch, size of pattern, needle size, colour or yarn. It can take a great many samples of swatches to finalise my idea of the right fabric. The successful design is also the 'right' balance of all the elements of colour, texture and pattern. This is a very personal feeling, and if you want to try out the method this is the point at which you have to rely on your own judgement and not be satisfied too easily with your efforts! Always push on a little further, with one more sample or stitch variation. The result of all this sampling in my own case is that I have generated a veritable mountain of swatches over a period of time – I do return to them and occasionally put one to good use again.

I like to experiment in my more graphic designs with the scale of the imagery on the garment and its effect on the body when worn. Sometimes it is surprising how flattering very large patterning can be, contrary to the 'correct' rules of dress, as you can see from some of my floral designs. On the other hand a small repeated motif works extremely well by creating an overall effect of pattern and colour. It is best not to have any preconceived ideas of what should and should not work, but try out ideas for yourself.

So many of the designs in this book are multicoloured that you may be wondering about the lack of plain sweaters and cardigans. Plain coloured garments which rely on good shapes and interesting stitches and textures for their effect are important in anyone's wardrobe, and easy to wear. You can knit up any of the shapes from the patterns in the book in a single colour for a basic, well proportioned garment which will be really useful – when you just feel like wearing one colour at a time! (Note that the quantities of yarn you need will have to take into account the allowance for the contrast colours in the original patterns.)

For example, for a plain mohair cardigan use the Curves, Iris or Fans patterns: the shapes are all very similar, but each has a different style of collar, and the Fans cardigan has useful pockets. Similarly, the Shield sweater or cardigan styles would look very good knitted in a single strong colour – just miss out all the coloured patterns and knit the body sections entirely in reverse stocking stitch. The Flower tunic is another style which adapts very easily and looks stunning in a primary colour.

I pay close attention to varying the shapes and details of the clothes for every new collection – this is an entirely natural process, not just related to fashion, as the eye tires of familiar proportions. A designer always has to move onto something new to satisfy his or her instincts. If you look at any very old clothes you have, especially sweaters, you will see the point quite clearly. Details such as collar shapes, type of ribbing, depth of edgings, size of armhole and so on all contribute to the overall proportions and look of any garment, and make older clothes look dated.

A good starting point for anyone wanting to design their own knitwear is to measure very carefully a favourite piece of clothing, and then to use these dimensions as a basis for working out the proportions you need. Once you have established your tension in the yarn you want to use, then you can begin the calculations for numbers of stitches and rows. Alternatively there are many shapes in this book which you could use or adapt to your own variations. If you use the shapes that work well for you and experiment with the motifs given, or alternative yarns and pattern variations, you will have endless potential to keep you engaged in knitting creatively for your own pleasure for quite some time.

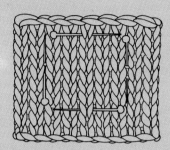

in a difference of one or even two sizes in the finished garment. When the knitting is worked on fairly large needles, say 5½mm (UK size 5) as are many of the designs in this book,

TECHNICAL SECTION

YARNS

The choice of yarn is of primary importance as it will govern the entire look and feel of the final results. The thickness of the yarn will determine the weight of the garment and whether it will knit up quickly or slowly. Mohair is an excellent yarn as it is very attractive in itself, and is lightweight but can be knitted on large needles.

Throughout the book I have used just four main types of yarns: 75% mohair, 100% angora, 100% wool of approximately aran weight and a textured 100% cotton of 4-ply (light) weight. Specific details are given with each pattern, but it is useful to note that they are all knitted on fairly large needles.

One of the advantages of using mohair and 100% angora is that they are interchangeable in many designs, for example Curves and Iris cardigans. The mohair I have used is the standard mohair widely available, but the 100% angora is very special, and not to be confused with finer angora mixture yarns containing about 70% angora which knit to a different tension.

When substituting yarns, the important thing is to match the tension. It will not be a successful substitute if the tension cannot be matched. Yarn quantities given in the patterns are based on average requirements and may vary slightly in individual cases.

TENSION

The word 'tension' ('gauge') when applied to the tightness or slackness of a piece of knitted fabric refers to the specific number of stitches and rows which can be counted within a given measurement, over a particular knitted stitch or pattern. Sometimes tension is quoted per inch/2½cm, or per 2in/5cm, but I always use the larger measurement of 4in/10cm because it gives more accurate results.

Accuracy is all important when measuring tension, because any errors will be multiplied over the entire garment. An innaccurate tension measurement can quite easily result

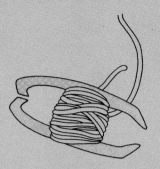

obviously extreme, but it is revealing that such a vast difference is possible.

The photograph of the white Vase of Flowers coat shows what can happen if you knit too loosely as this particular coat has been. However, it is still extremely wearable, and looks even more luxurious for being large.

A small additional point – after taking great care to to get the correct tension for the body of your knitting, don't forget to ensure that your cast on and cast off edges are loose enough to stretch with the main knitting, especially around neck edges.

If you are ever in doubt about your tension checking, here are a few points which will help you avoid too many mistakes.

It is generally better to be knitting slightly loose rather than slightly tight, so choose the larger sized needles if you are unsure between two sizes. This means a slightly large but wearable garment rather than one which is just too small.

If you simply cannot match both the stitches tension given and the rows tension because your knitting is differently proportioned, then aim to match the stitches tension for accurate width, and the length can generally be adjusted longer or shorter at some stage of the pattern.

Finally, remember to check your knitting against the measurement diagrams as you go along – this will point up any problems at an early stage. Don't make the mistake of knitting to the end and hoping for magic at the making up stage!

Variations in tension can be deliberately used to advantage in order to change the size of a garment, without having to change the pattern instructions. This is particularly useful when the design is worked entirely from charts, or when it is important for the pattern to be matched at the side seams. The whole garment can then be made larger or smaller in porportion. This technique is not suitable for every design, however, as the knitting itself must not become too loose or too tight. An example of this sizing technique can be found in the Heraldic section.

WORKING WITH MANY COLOURS

Many of the patterns in the book are knitted using several colours together in the same row. This requires a little preliminary organisation and can then be managed without too much frustrating tangling of colours.

Reference is often made in the patterns to winding 'bobbins' of colours, or 'butterfly twists' of yarn. Commercially available bobbins are made of plastic usually in the shape of a flat letter H, with a slit to hold the end of yarn firmly. You can easily make the same sort of bobbin yourself out of stiff card. Wind a bobbin of yarn for each separate section of colour across the row. (There will

often be several bobbins in each colour.) Then keep all the bobbins close to the needle as you are working, just unravelling small amounts as required.

The same principle applies to using 'butterfly twists' or finger skeins of yarn, which are a little easier to handle where there are a great many colours. To make these, start with the end of yarn in the palm of the hand, and wind it in a figure-of-eight around thumb and little finger. Fasten by wrapping the end of yarn around the centre and securing, then work from the loose end left at the **beginning**. The

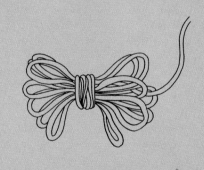

Crossing yarns – knit side

yarn pulls out from the centre of the skein and does not unravel during knitting.

For very small areas of colour, simply measure out a sufficient length of yarn and leave this hanging free.

When changing from one colour to the next

the size of each individual stitch is quite significant, and half or even quarter stitches must be taken into account.

Never skip the stage of checking your tension – you cannot assume that your knitting is the same as that given in the pattern, especially over special stitches. The given tension in my patterns is based on the average results from tests with many knitters, but individual knitting can vary widely.

Do not deceive yourself when measuring tension – it will definitely lead to disappointing results. Avoid stretching or distorting your work, and do not press it unless the instructions say so. The method I give of pinning out then measuring is easier and more accurate than counting and measuring at the same time.

Your tension governs the size of the finished garment. If you knit tighter than the stated tension, the garment will be too small; if you knit looser, the garment will be too large. If, for example, the pattern specifies 16 stitches to 4in/10cm but you knit 17 stitches to 4in, over a back piece with 80 stitches, the back will be 1¼in/3cm too narrow. If this is repeated on the front it will result in a 2½in/6cm difference overall, i.e. it will be a whole size smaller. This shows how even a small error in tension can make a great difference in size – and of course it affects the length as well as the width. You can see the principle illustrated from the photograph of the child's size Fairisle Fun design. The point I am making is that this is not in fact a children's size, but the adult size pattern knitted at drastically the wrong tension! This is always cross the yarns on the wrong side of the work to link the colours. To do this, simply drop the first colour, then pick up the new colour by taking it from underneath the first one so the two strands cross each other and link together. If the colours are not linked in this way, a hole is created.

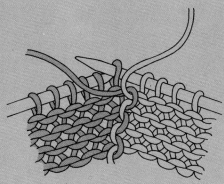

Crossing yarns – purl side

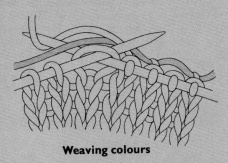

Weaving colours

Most of the colour work in the book is knitted in stocking stitch, but if you are changing colours in any other stitch, just ensure that you take the yarns to the wrong side before crossing them, then continue in pattern.

Note that when working a fairisle with two colours, the colour not in use should be stranded loosely across the back over not more than four stitches. If the colour has to be stranded over more than four stitches then weave it in at the back of the work, taking it over and under the first colour.

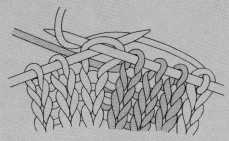

Stranding colours

FOLLOWING GRAPH CHARTS

The pattern graph is an exact representation of the garment piece or section to be knitted, showing every stitch and row and including all the shaping required. Once understood, the charts are very easy to follow, and it is easier to keep your place than it is in a set of written instructions.

Although detailed explanation of the shaping is given in each pattern, it is possible to read all the shaping directly from the chart itself. The charts are read row by row, starting at the bottom right, in alternating directions. Odd numbered rows are read from right to left, even numbered rows from left to right. They are usually, but not always, worked in stocking stitch. Each square of the chart represents one stitch. Each stitch is worked in the colour indicated, either by a symbol or by a key letter within an outlined area. If the design is knitted in stocking stitch, odd numbered rows are knit, even numbered rows are purl. If the design is worked in another stitch, then odd numbered rows are right side rows, even numbered rows are wrong side rows.

Use a separate ball or length of yarn for each area of colour, and cross the yarns when changing colour to link the colours and prevent holes (see paragraph above).

To follow shaping from the chart: When the outline moves horizontally across one square, this represents a single increase or decrease at the beginning and/or end of the numbered row to be worked next. When the outline moves horizontally across 2 or more squares, this represents a number of stitches to be cast on or off at the beinning of the numbered row.

It is sometimes useful to be able to work a pattern in reverse, perhaps to match the design at the shoulders. Instead of redrawing the chart in reverse, simply work from the chart in reverse, by making odd numbered rows wrong side rows, and even numbered rows right side rows instead. The chart is followed in exactly the same way, but right side and wrong side are interchanged. This principle is used in the Fairisle Fun cardigan. Although the graph charts are drawn on squared paper, the actual proportions of knitted stitches are not square. There are generally more rows than stitches in a given measurement, as you can see from the tension. If you are designing a motif on squared paper to be knitted, then allowance must be made for this, by making your image longer on the drawn chart. This can be quite hard to visualise, but specially proportioned graph paper is now available which makes the process easier, as its 'squares' correspond to the knitted stitch proportions.

EMBROIDERY

Simple embroidery techniques can be very effective to add highlights and finishing touches to a design. I like to use French knots to add small amounts of colour, and chain stitch to create lines which would be tricky to knit in. These effects also add textural interest to a flat surface. Use a large-eyed needle with a rounded point to avoid splitting the yarn.

To work French knots, secure the yarn with a backstitch, insert the needle again and wrap the yarn several times around its point, pull the needle through the loops and finish with a backstitch. Experiment with the number of

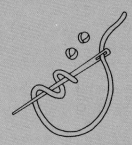

turns around the needle to give the right effect, I prefer to do many turns to give a long 'caterpillar' effect; fewer turns will produce a rounder knot.

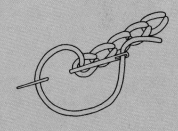

Chain stitch can be worked in two ways, using either a needle or a crochet hook.

For the needle method, start by securing a length of yarn, take the needle through the knitting to make a stitch, then wrap the yarn once under the point of the needle. Hold the loop with your thumb and pull the needle through. Put the needle in again for the next stitch in the same place as the yarn inside the chain loop, and repeat the procedure, following the desired line. Secure the last loop with a small stitch.

For the crochet hook method, the yarn is held underneath the knitting throughout. Insert the crochet hook through the fabric from the right side and draw the yarn through the knitting to the right side. With the yarn still around the hook, put the hook through the fabric again a little further ahead, and draw a new loop through the fabric and then the loop already on the hook. One loop remains on the hook. Repeat the process. This method takes a little practice, but is quicker to work and avoids having to join in separate lengths of yarn at regular intervals as in the needle method. It is best to hold the yarn fairly taut under the knitting so it is easier to catch with the hook.

With either method, ensure you do not pull the chain stitches too tight, as the lines must retain the same elasticity as the knitted fabric you are working on.

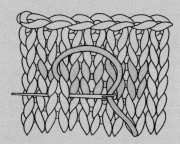

Another very useful method of embroidering onto knitting is Swiss Darning (Duplicate stitch). This stitch exactly copies the knitted stitches and is most effective worked on stocking stitch. It can be used for large or small areas and avoids the need to knit in separate colours for small details. However, when worked over large areas, the effect is not as neat as knitting in the colour. Best results are obtained if the embroidery is worked from the top of the area in rows to the bottom.

To work the stitch, use the same yarn as the knitted fabric, or one slightly thicker. If a finer yarn is used, the background will show through. Starting at the base of the first stitch to be covered, bring the needle through from back to front. Insert the needle from right to left behind the base of the stitch above, then back into the base of the first stitch from front to back. Do not pull the yarn too tight, just try to match the size of the existing stitches. Bring the needle to the front again through the base of the next stitch to be covered and repeat. Note that the new yarn follows exactly the same path as the stitches of the knitting itself.

I sometimes use a slight variation on standard Swiss Darning as described above, which is quicker to work. I call it Elongated Swiss Darning, and work it in the same manner, except that 2 or more knitted stitches in a vertical line are covered with one embroidered stitch, which becomes elongated. This method does not cover the knitting so densely, and avoids any tendency to distort, which can occur when heavy yarns are being used. The Rosette sweater incorporates this technique.

FINISHING

Finishing includes all those processes which turn your knitted pieces into a wearable garment: pressing, neatening, and seaming. Follow the instructions on the ball bands or given in the pattern with regard to pressing. The mohair and angora yarns used in the book do not require pressing; the wool and cotton yarns should be steam pressed, using a steam iron or a damp cloth with a dry iron. Never press too heavily as this results in a lifeless fabric. Most fine yarns require little more than a passing over with steam, without ever pressing onto the knitting. Heavier wools such as the Wool Twist require more steam to set them. Cabled and ribbed edgings must not be pressed as this destroys their elasticity. Use the layout diagrams as a guide to the size of each piece, and pin them out to correspond.

If the knitting is multicoloured, there will inevitably be loose ends where colours have been joined in and broken off. The way you deal with these is up to you, whether you darn them in neatly, leave them hanging or tie knots. The only important part is to close up the small gaps which appear when a new yarn is joined in by threading the needle and linking the yarn through the adjacent stitch. With a little forward thinking, these can be knitted in as you work, however, if the pattern is very detailed, you may prefer to leave the ends of yarn to be dealt with later. Wherever possible, darn the ends into a seam

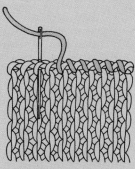

Oversewn seam

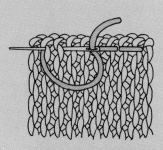

Backstitch seam

after joining the pieces. If the loose ends are in the centre of the pieces, then I recommend darning them in working up and down and not across the width, to prevent them pulling

Edge to edge seam

out when the knitting is stretched. Always darn in a sufficient length for the same reason.

As a general rule I recommend backstitch for seaming the garment pieces, because of the neat appearance it gives, and it does not require perfect edges. The loose ends of yarn can then be darned into the seam on the inside. However the cuffs, waistbands and collars are usually neat enough to be joined with an edge to edge seam for less bulk.

LININGS

To make the jackets and coats featured in the book even more special, it is possible to line them with fabric which gives them a better drape and makes them really glamorous. I have used silk linings for the pure angora and mohair coats and crepe satin fabric for the heavier wool coats.

You will need approximately 2 yards/metres of fabric to line a jacket and 3 yards/metres for a coat. Before making up the knitting, use the knitted pieces in conjunction with the layout diagrams to make a pattern. You will need to add large seam allowances and particularly allow extra length, because the knitting will drop slightly compared to the lining. Make up the jacket or coat and its lining separately and then put the two together, wrong sides inside. Pin together all around the shoulders, neck and front edges, and around the armholes. Insert any shoulder pads at this stage. Carefully sew the lining to the knitting, taking it just inside the edgings. To help you in achieving the correct drape, hang the piece up and keep trying it on to check. You can leave the straight bottom edge of a jacket loose, but attach the bottom edge of a coat lining to the coat, allowing some extra length. It is better to allow too much fabric than too little as excess may be taken in with pleats or tucks if necessary.

READING THE PATTERNS

Measurements are given first in inches, then centimetres. It is best to follow either one set of figures or the other.

Where there is more than one size, the larger sizes are in square brackets. If only one figure is stated, then this applies to all sizes. Instructions given in round brackets should be repeated the number of times stated immediately after the brackets.

NOTES FOR MACHINE KNITTERS

For me, both hand and machine knitting are different means to the same end – that of creating beautiful and exciting knitwear. The graphic nature of my designs, means that most of them can be knitted either by hand or by machine. However, this does not imply that the process is fully automatic – far from it! The intarsia technique which I use has to be worked manually on the machine, with every colour individually laid across the needles by hand.

Over two thirds of the designs in the book can be translated to machine knitting, using a chunky gauge machine. All the yarns used knit very easily on this coarse gauge, but they *cannot* be knitted on standard gauge machines. It is not necessary to have a ribbing attachment, because the best results are achieved by handknitting the edgings onto the machine knit pieces.

As with hand knitting, tension is of the utmost importance. The main point to understand when attempting any translation is how the tension and therefore proportions differ between hand knit and machine knit. This of course depends on the yarn used, but the general principle is that chunky gauge machine knitting produces fewer stitches and more rows to the 4in/10cm than does hand knitting (see below).

The angora, wool and cotton yarns used in the book produce a very good handle when machine knitted. As with all hairy yarns, the mohair yarn becomes a little flattened when machine knitted, but provided it is knitted loosely enough, it can be brushed gently to restore its characteristic hairy texture. The angora yarn does not require brushing as the hairs will burst out when the pieces are handled.

Any of the designs which are knitted from charts in stocking stitch can be adapted to the intarsia technique. These include many of the mohair designs such as Fans, Curves, Rectangles, and Iris, plus wool designs such as the Stained Glass sweater and Small Shields, and the cotton Matisse dress.

Other designs are also adaptable using different techniques, for example the Bobbly Grid. It is only possible to to give pointers to all these adaptations here, and discuss the general methods.

Take the mohair designs, for example Rectangles. First we must establish a tension for our machine knitted mohair. This must be done by knitting a sample using the intarsia technique (which is described in the machine manual), as it will be different from basic stocking stitch. I have found that knitting at a loose tension (between 8 and 9 on the tension dial) produces a nice fabric giving a tension of 15 sts and 23 rows to 4in/10cm. When we compare this to the handknit tension of 16 sts and 20 rows to 4in/10cm, we can see that we have fewer stitches and more rows, so if we were to knit from the chart as it stands, the pieces would be slightly wider and shorter than intended. There are 108 rows to the chart for back and front, which, on the handknit calculation of 5 rows to 1in/2½cm, measures 21½in/54cm. Our machine knit tension of 23 rows to 4in/10cm would only give a length of 18¾in/47cm, which is 2¾in/7cm shorter. Clearly this has to be compensated for by knitting extra rows: we need 3 extra for every 20 of the chart to bring the length back to the original, that is 16 rows extra. These extra rows must be evenly divided up the length of the piece to keep the proportions correct. The simplest way to do this without having to draw a new chart, is to mark 16 individual rows on the chart, spaced out evenly between the top and bottom (avoiding the neck and armhole shaping for simplicity). Then simply knit these marked rows twice. This will have virtually no effect on the pattern itself but will restore the length. The same principle can be applied to the sleeve, just remember not to alter the shaping on the extra rows. As the sleeve chart is only 92 rows we will only need 13 additional rows to make up the length.

If using this technique, you must remember that the row numbers will not match the ones on the chart unless you stop your row counter at each extra row.

Regarding the width, you could decide to leave it as the original chart and have a sweater about 1¼in/3cm wider in the body. Or alternatively, you could reduce the stitches by one stitch for every 16, that is by 5 sts.

As all the mohair stocking stitch designs are based on the same tension, this calculation could be applied to all the others in the same way. The principle of stretching out the chart by repeating rows works even for a pattern such as the Iris. If you prefer, you could add plain rows to top and bottom where the design permits.

Calculations like this are not always necessary. If the hand and machine knit tensions are very similar, you can simply knit up the design to the original pattern. But you will still need to do a little calculating (after knitting your tension square) in order to predict what the difference in length and width will be.

Another method of adapting ideas in the book is to take a motif or pattern and use that within an existing machine knitting pattern of your own. Bobbles are made by knitting backwards and forwards a few times over 2 or 3 needles, using a contrast colour, and can be positioned anywhere on a plain base to form regular or random designs.

I hope these ideas indicate that there is equal scope for designs such as these in machine knitting, using the machine in conjunction with your own manual skills.

ABBREVIATIONS

k = knit p = purl
st(s) = stitch(es)
st st = stocking stitch (1 row k, 1 row p) (US: stockinette stitch)
rev st st = reverse stocking stitch (1 row p, 1 row k)
g st = garter stitch (every row k)
beg = beginning tog = together
cont = continue(ing)
alt = alternate (every other)
foll = following rep = repeat
inc = increase(ing) dec = decrease(ing)
rem = remain(ing)
patt = pattern
sl = slip
sl 1k = slip one knitwise
sl 1p = slip one purlwise
psso = pass slip stitch over
yfwd = yarn forward   yb = yarn back
yrn = yarn round needle
in = inch(es)
cm = centimetres   mm = millmetres
ws = wrong side rs = right side
approx = approximately
no = number col = colour
c4b = cable 4 back: slip next 2 sts onto cable needle and leave at back of work, k2, k2 sts from cable needle.
c4f = cable 4 front: slip next 2 sts onto cable needle and leave at front of work, k2, k2 sts from cable needle.
tw2 = twist 2: knit into front of 2nd st, knit into frontof first st, slip both sts off left hand needle together.
dc = double crochet (single crochet)

KNITTING NEEDLES

Metric (in mm)	Britain	USA
9	000	15
8½	00	13
8	0	–
7½	1	11
7	2	10½
6½	3	10
6	4	9
5½	5	8
5	6	7
4½	7	6
4	8	5
3½ and 3¾	9	4
3¼	10	3
2¾ and 3	11	2
2½	12	1
2¼	13	0
2	14	00

Section I
GRAPHIC

THE GEOMETRIC, ABSTRACT AND LINEAR DE-
SIGNS IN THIS GROUP USE IDEAS WHICH ARE
BASICALLY SIMPLE, SO COLOUR PLAYS A VERY
IMPORTANT PART. EACH DESIGN CAN BE GIVEN
A TOTALLY NEW LOOK IF THE COLOUR PALETTE
IS CHANGED, FOR EXAMPLE BY CHOOSING
CLOSE SHADES OF ONE OR TWO COLOURS,
INSTEAD OF BRIGHT CONTRASTS.

MANY OF THE DESIGNS IN THE FOLLOWING
PAGES ARE CARRIED OUT IN STOCKING STITCH
WHICH GIVES ME THE FREEDOM TO DESIGN ON
GRAPH PAPER AND CONCENTRATE ON PAT-
TERN, SHAPE AND COLOUR INSTEAD.

I HAVE CHOSEN TO MAKE MOST OF THE DESIGNS
IN THIS SECTION IN MOHAIR OR TEXTURED
COTTON TO GIVE TEXTURAL INTEREST AND
DEPTH TO THE SURFACE, SO SOFTENING THE
GRAPHIC LINES.

THE IDEA OF LINES TRAVELLING OVER THE
BODY IS SIMPLE AND VERY EFFECTIVE. IN THE
BOBBLY GRID CARDIGAN THE LINES ARE
FORMED BY BOBBLES KNITTED IN ACROSS THE
SURFACE. THE METHOD COULD ALSO BE USED
TO CREATE DIAMONDS, DIAGONALS, CIRCLES
OR MANY OTHER SHAPES.

CHECKED PATTERNS ARE SO CLASSIC THEY
NEVER GO OUT OF FASHION – I HAVE INCLUDED
TWO DESIGNS ON THIS THEME, ONE USING AN
OVERSIZED DOGTOOTH CHECK AND THE OTHER
BASED ON A TARTAN EFFECT.

IN THE GEOMETRIC DESIGNS, SUCH AS TRI-
ANGLES AND RECTANGLES, THE EMPHASIS IS ON
THE DIVISION OF THE WHOLE SURFACE INTO
SMALLER AREAS WHICH ARE THEN COLOURED.

GEOMETRIC LINES AND PATTERNS TAKE ON A
NEW DIMENSION WHEN ACTUALLY WORN. ONE
OF THE MOST POPULAR OF ALL MY DESIGNS IS
THE FAIRISLE FUN SWEATER. IN THIS SWEATER
I WANTED TO BREAK AWAY FROM THE TRADI-
TIONAL HORIZONTAL BANDS OF FAIRISLE PAT-
TERNS, SO I CREATED A STRONG DIAGONAL LINE
ACROSS THE BODY, AND TRANSLATED IT INTO
MOHAIR TO GIVE SOMETHING COMPLETELY
FRESH. THE IDEA WORKS EQUALLY WELL WHEN
USED ON A SMALLER SCALE IN THE SUMMER
CARDIGAN VERSION. THE COLOURS NEED TO
BE WELL BALANCED IN TONE TO GIVE A
HARMONIOUS EFFECT.

A PART OF THE GRAPHIC DESIGN PROCESS I
ENJOY IS TRANSLATING DRAWN CURVES INTO
THE STEPPED OUTLINE OF A GRAPH PATTERN,
AND THE CURVES CARDIGAN IS A FAVOURITE
DESIGN IN THIS CATEGORY.

ONE OF THE GREAT MASTERS OF GRAPHIC
IMAGERY IS MATISSE, WHOSE COLLAGE 'CUT-
OUTS' HAVE INSPIRED THE SUMMER DRESS I
HAVE NAMED AFTER HIM. THIS DRESS WAS
GREAT FUN TO DESIGN AND CAN ONLY BE FUN
TO WEAR!

BOBBLY GRID

The cardigan is knitted in Mohair in stocking stitch with contrast bobbles knitted in grid formation.

SIZES
There are 2 sizes to fit up to 36in/91cm or up to 38in/97cm bust.
Knitted measurements: all round width at underarm 39[41]in/99[104]cm including front bands; length 22[22½]in/56[57]cm; sleeve length 22½[23]in/57[58½]cm.

ABBREVIATIONS
See page 15.

MATERIALS
○ 25 × 25g balls of Mohair in 9 colours as follows:
    17 balls in main colour (MC)
    1 ball each of 8 contrast colours (C)
○ 6 buttons
○ 2 pairs of needles are required, one pair for main parts in size to give correct tension; one pair 3 sizes smaller for ribbing

TENSION
Measured over st st, 16 sts and 20 rows to 4in/10cm using 5½mm (UK size 5) needles, or the size to give correct tension. Recommended needles for ribbing: 4mm (UK size 8).
A grid 'square' measures 4in/10cm wide by 3in/7½cm deep from centre to centre of bobble lines.
To avoid disappointment, it is essential to check your tension carefully before commencing the garment and use the needles which give **you** the correct tension. **This may not be the size quoted in the standard tension**, as individual knitters vary.
How to check tension: Using the recommended needles and a light colour, cast on 24 sts and work in st st for 30 rows. Cast off. Pin the square down flat without stretching. Place a pin between 2 sts near the left, count 16 sts and mark with another pin between the 16th and 17th sts. Mark out 20 rows in the same way. Measure the distance between pins. This should be 4in/10cm in both directions. If it is less your knitting is too tight – try one size larger needle. If it is more, your knitting is too loose – try one size smaller needle. Repeat the process until the correct tension is achieved. Do not be afraid to go up or down more than one needle size. Adjust the size of the second pair of needles accordingly.

NOTES ON WORKING PATTERN
Bobbles: bobbles are made on knit rows only as follows: using C, knit into front and back of next st (2 loops). Turn and k2, turn and p2, pass the 2nd C st over the first. Slip rem C st onto the other needle and knit in MC (abbreviated mb = make bobble).
Bobble Grid pattern: bobbles are made on all rs (knit) rows, on alt sts for horizontal lines and alt rows for vertical lines. There are 6 bobbles (13 sts) between vertical lines, and 7 bobbles (15 rows) between horizontal lines. Patt repeats over 14 sts and 16 rows. Each bobble is a different col, using all 8 contrast cols randomly. Break yarn after each bobble, leaving ends of approx 2in/5cm for fastening off. It is helpful to prepare lengths of contrast cols first, then use these at random, thus avoiding balls of yarn entangling.

BACK
Using the smaller needles and MC, cast on 69[73] sts and work in k1, p1 rib for 1in/2½cm. Change to the larger needles and purl 1 row, inc 1 st at beg and end of row. 71[75] sts. Commence patt as follows:
1st patt row (rs): k14[2]MC, mb, (k13MC, mb) 3[5] times, k14[2]MC.
2nd and all ws rows: purl in MC.
Repeat these 2 rows 6 times more (7 bobbles in vertical lines). Work first horizontal line of bobbles as follows:
Row 15: k2MC, mb, (k1MC, mb) 33[35] times, k2MC.
Row 16: purl in MC.
Row 1–16 form the patt. Cont straight until work measures 13[13½]in/33[34½]cm from beg.
Shape armholes: cast off 3 sts at beg of next 4 rows. Dec 1 st at beg of next 6 rows. 53[57] sts. Cont in patt without shaping until back measures 20½[21¼]in/52[54]cm from beg.
Shape shoulders: cast off 4 sts at beg of next 6[4] rows, and 5 sts at beg of next 2[4] rows. Cast off rem 19[21] sts.

RIGHT FRONT
Pocket lining: using the larger needles and MC, cast on 13 sts and work in st st for 9in/23cm, to be used double. Leave on a stitch holder or spare needle. Using the smaller needles and MC, cast on 33[35] sts and work in k1, p1 rib for 1in/2½cm. Change to the larger needles and purl 1 row, inc 1 st at beg and end of row. 35[37] sts. *Commence patt as follows:
Row 1(rs): k8MC, mb, k13MC, mb, k12[14]MC.
Row 2: purl in MC.
Repeat these 2 rows 6 times more.
Row 15: k2MC, (mb, k1MC) 16[17] times, k1MC.
Row 16: purl in MC.
Repeat first 2 rows of patt then work pocket band as follows:
Row 19: k8MC, mb, rib 13MC, mb, k12[14]MC.
Row 20: p13[15]MC, rib 13MC, p9MC.
Repeat last 2 rows twice more.

Divide for pocket: k8MC, mb, with MC cast off next 13 sts ribwise, sl last st back onto left-hand needle, break yarn. With rs facing, rejoin MC and k 13 sts from pocket lining, mb, k12[14]MC.
Cont straight in patt until front matches back to armhole, ending with a rs row.
Shape armhole: cast off 3 sts at beg of next row, and 2 sts at beg of foll alt row. Dec 1 st at armhole edge of foll 2 alt rows. 28[30] sts. Patt 2 rows.
Shape neck: dec 1 st at centre front edge of next and every foll alt row until 17[18] sts rem. Cont straight until armhole matches back, ending with a rs row.
Shape shoulder: cast off 4 sts at beg of next and foll 2[1] alt rows. Cast off 5 sts at beg of foll 1[2] alt rows.

LEFT FRONT
Work as right to *. Commence patt as follows:
Row 1: k12[14]MC, mb, k13MC, mb, k8MC.
Row 2: purl in MC.
Cont in patt, working as reverse of right front, and reversing shaping by ending with ws rows before shaping.

SLEEVES
Using the smaller needles and MC, cast on 39[41] sts and work in k1, p1 rib for 1in/2½cm. Change to the larger needles and purl 1 row. Commence patt as follows:
Row 1: k12[13]MC, mb, k13MC, mb, k12[13]MC.
Row 2: purl in MC.
Row 3: inc. in first st, k11[12]MC, mb, k13MC, mb, k11[12]MC, inc in last st. 41[43] sts.
Cont in patt as set, with 2 vertical lines only up centre of sleeve, inc 1 st at each end of rs rows until there are 7 bobbles vertically, ending with a purl row. 51[53] sts.
Row 15: (k1MC, mb) 25[26] times, k1MC.
Row 16: purl in MC.
These 16 rows form the pattern. Cont in patt, inc 1 st at each side of every 12th row to 57[59] sts, working extra bobbles into horizontal lines of grid patt as necessary. Work straight until sleeve measures 15½[16]in/39½[40½]cm from beg. (Adjust sleeve length at this point if desired.)
Shape top: cast off 3 sts at beg of next 2 rows. Cont straight in patt until sleeve measures 20½[21]in/52[53½]cm from beg. Dec 1 st at each end of every foll row until 29[31] sts remain. (Sleeve measures 22½[23]in/57 [58½]cm.) Cast off.

FRONT EDGINGS AND COLLAR
Knitted throughout in k1, p1 rib using the smaller needles and MC, and worked in one piece starting at bottom edge of right front. Cast on 12 sts and work as follows:
Row 1(rs): sl 1k, p1, (k1, p1) 5 times.

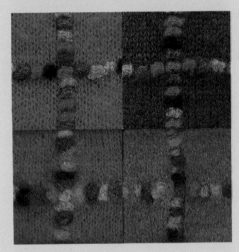

Row 2 (ws): (k1, p1) 6 times.
Repeat these 2 rows once. Make first buttonhole:

Next row: sl 1k, p1, k1, p2 tog, yrn, rib to end.

Cont straight in rib, slipping first st of rs rows (outer edge) and making 5 more buttonholes at intervals of $2\frac{3}{4}$in/7cm. At the same time, when work measures $10\frac{1}{2}$[11]in/26$\frac{1}{2}$[28]cm, shape **inside** edge only by inc 1 st on next and every foll 3rd row until there are 25 sts. Mark inside edge with a coloured thread. Cont straight until work measures $21\frac{1}{2}$[22]in/ 54$\frac{1}{2}$[56]cm ending with a ws row (at outer edge).

Shape collar: cast off 13 sts at beg of next row. Work 1 row. Inc 1 st at beg of next and every foll alt row until there are 18 sts. Cont straight until work measures $27\frac{1}{2}$[28]in/ 70[71]cm from beg, ending with a ws row. Shape second side as reverse of first side, starting as follows:

Dec 1 st at beg of next and every foll alt row until 12 sts rem, ending with a ws row. Cast on 13 sts at beg of next row and cont straight until work measures same as first side to coloured thread. Complete to correspond with first side, omitting buttonholes.

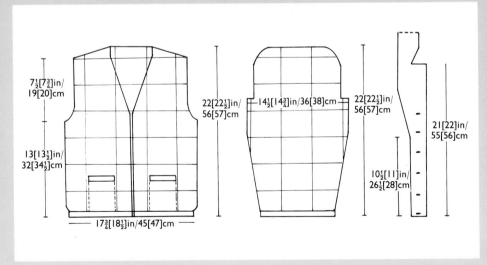

$7\frac{1}{2}$[$7\frac{3}{4}$]in/ 19[20]cm

13[$13\frac{1}{2}$]in/ 32[34$\frac{1}{2}$]cm

$17\frac{3}{4}$[$18\frac{1}{2}$]in/45[47]cm

22[$22\frac{1}{2}$]in/ 56[57]cm

$14\frac{1}{2}$[$14\frac{3}{4}$]in/36[38]cm

22[$22\frac{1}{2}$]in/ 56[57]cm

21[22]in/ 55[56]cm

$10\frac{1}{2}$[11]in/ 26$\frac{1}{2}$[28]cm

FINISHING

Do not press. Darn in or securely tie off ends on inside of work. Using backstitch seams, join shoulders, side and sleeve seams. Set in sleeves, easing fullness to the top of sleeve. Pin front band around front and necé edges, aligning points of collar to shoulder seams. Oversew in position from the inside. Sew on buttons. Stitch lower edge of each pocket lining to base of pocket band, backstitch sides of pocket linings.

19

DOGTOOTH JACKET

The dogtooth check is a classic pattern originally found in woven fabrics, and works extremely well when scaled up and knitted in Mohair. The choice of colour is yours – use either strong contrasts as in the sweater, or more subtle combinations, such as the black and grey of the jacket shown. Both are knitted in fairisle with ribbed edgings. The jacket is worked in only three main pieces – the sleeves and body are knitted all in one which requires the use of a circular needle. The sweater can equally be worn by a man – you will only need to adjust the sleeve and body lengths to fit.

SIZES

Two sizes to fit up to 36in/91cm or up to 38in/97cm bust.

Knitted measurements: all round width at underarm 39½[44]in/100[112]cm; length 24[24½]in/61[62]cm.

ABBREVIATIONS

See page 15.

MATERIALS

○ 14[15] × 25g balls of Mohair in main colour (A)
○ 9[10] × 25g balls of Mohair in contrast colour (B)
○ 3 large buttons
○ 2 pairs of needles are required, one pair for main parts in fairisle in size to give correct tension, one pair 2 sizes smaller for ribbing and collar
○ 1 circular needle in larger size
○ 2 stitch holders
○ medium crochet hook

TENSION

Measured over dogtooth check patt, 18 sts and 18 rows to 4in/10cm, using 6mm (UK size 4) needles or the size to give the correct tension. Recommended needles for ribbing: 5mm (UK size 6).

To avoid disappointment, it is essential to check your tension carefully before commencing the garment and use the needles which give you the correct tension. **This may not be the size quoted in the standard tension** as individual knitters vary.

How to check tension: using the recommended needles and the 2 colours A & B, work dogtooth check patt, as follows: (NB: weave in col not in use **loosely** at the back every 3rd or 4th st and take care not to pull too tight):

Cast on 30 sts (patt rep over 10 sts and 10 rows).

Row 1 (rs): knit *5A, 2B, 2A, 1B, rep from *.
Rows 2(ws): purl *2B, 2A, 1B, 5A, rep from *.
Row 3: knit *7A, 2B, 1A, rep from *.
Row 4: purl *1A, 3B, 6A, rep from *.

Row 5: knit *5A, 3B, 2A, rep from *.
Row 6: purl *5B, 1A, 2B, 2A, rep from *.
Row 7: knit *1A, 2B, 2A, 5B, rep from *.
Row 8: purl *6B, 2A, 2B, rep from *.
Row 9: knit *1B, 3A, 6B, rep from *.
Row 10: purl *7B, 3A, rep from *.
Rep rows 1–10 twice more. Cast off loosely. Pin the square down flat without stretching. Place a pin between 2 sts near the left, count 18 sts and mark with another pin between the 18th and 19th sts. Mark out 18 rows in the same way. Measure the distance between pins. This should be 4in/10cm in both directions. If it is less your knitting is too tight – try one size larger needle. If it is more, your knitting is too loose – try one size smaller needle. Repeat the process until the correct tension is achieved. Do not be afraid to go up or down more than one needle size. Adjust the size of the second pair of needles accordingly.

NOTES ON WORKING PATTERN

Small charts of patt repeat are given as guidance. One square of chart represents one stitch. Odd numbered rows (rs) are knit – read from right to left; even numbered rows (ws) are purl – read from left to right. Weave in colour not in use loosely at the back of every 3rd or 4th st. Take care not to pull the colours at the back too tight as this will distort the knitting.

BACK

Using the larger needles and A, cast on 90[100] sts, join in B and work in patt starting from row 1, for 7[7½]in/18[19]cm.

Shape sleeves: keeping continuity of patt, cast on 10 sts at beg of next 18 rows. (Change to the circular needle as sts increase.) 270[280] sts. Cont in rows back and forth without shaping until work measures 16½[17]in/42[43]cm from beg.

Shape sleeve and shoulders: cast off 10 sts at beg of next 16 rows. Cast off 20 sts at beg of next 2 rows. Cast off 25[30] sts at beg of next 2 rows. Cast off rem 20 sts.

RIGHT FRONT

Using the larger needles and A, cast on 35[40] sts. Join in B and work 8[10] rows in patt, starting at row 1, working an additional half patt rep (for first size only) at beg of knit rows

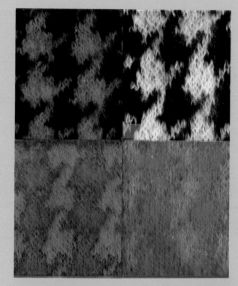

and end of purl rows – see chart for guidance. (On knit rows, work the extra 5 sts from 2nd half of patt; on purl rows, work the extra 5 sts from 1st half of patt.)

Divide for pocket: (rs facing) patt 15 sts, turn and leave rem 20[25] sts on a holder. Cont in patt for 17 rows more, starting at row 10[2] thus ending on a 6th[8th] patt row. Break yarn. Leave these sts on a holder, and return to the 20[25] sts for second side of pocket opening, rs facing. Rejoin yarn to inside edge and cast on 15sts in A for pocket lining. Working on these 35[40] sts work 18 rows in patt, starting at row 9[1], thus ending

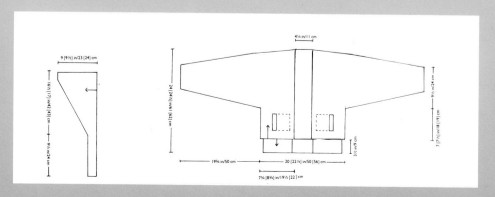

on a 6th [8th] patt row.

Next row: cast off 15 sts of pocket lining and break yarn. Slip the st rem after cast-off onto left-hand needle. Place 15 sts from holder onto left-hand needle and patt across all 35 [40] sts, working from row 7 [9] of patt. Patt until front matches back to start of sleeve shaping, ending with a rs row.

Shape sleeve: (ws facing) cast on 10 sts at beg of next and every foll alt row until 125 [130] sts. Cont straight until front matches back to start of sleeve and shoulder shaping, ending with a rs row.

Shape sleeve and shoulder: cast off 10 sts at beg of next and every foll alt row, 8 times in all. Cast off 20 sts at beg of foll alt row, work 1 row, cast off rem 25 [30] sts.

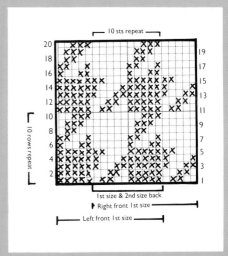

LEFT FRONT

Using the larger needles and A, cast on 35 [40] sts. Join in B and work the first 8 [10] rows of patt, working the extra half patt (for first size only) at end of all knit rows and beg of all purl rows – see chart for guidance. (On knit rows, work the extra 5 sts from 1st half of patt; on purl rows work the extra 5 sts from 2nd half of patt.)

Divide for pocket: patt 20 [25] sts and turn, leave rem 15 sts on a holder. Cast on 15 sts and cont in patt for 16 rows, thus ending on a 5th [7th] patt row. Cast off 15 sts at beg of next row, patt to end, leave sts on a holder. Return to sts for second side of pocket opening, rs facing, rejoin yarn to inside edge and patt 18 rows, starting at row 9 [1], and ending with a 6th [8th] patt row. Break yarn.

Next row: (rs facing) replace 20 [25] sts from holder onto same needle, rejoin yarn and patt across all 35 [40] sts working from row 7 [9] of patt. Cont until front matches back to start of sleeve shaping, ending with a ws row.

Shape sleeve: (rs facing) complete to correspond with right front.

Pocket bands: using the smaller needles and A, rs facing, knit up 18 sts along front edge of pocket opening. Work 7 rows in k1, p1 rib,

cast off loosely in rib. Oversew short ends securely to fronts.

COLLAR AND FRONT BANDS

Worked in two halves in k1, p1 rib throughout, using A and smaller needles.

Left half: cast on 141 [145] sts.

Rows 1 & 2: starting k1, rib 20, turn, sl 1, rib to end.

Rows 3 & 4: rib 24, turn, sl 1, rib to end.

Rows 5 & 6: rib 28, turn, sl 1, rib to end.

Rows 7 & 8: rib 32, turn, sl 1, rib to end.

Rows 9 & 10: rib 36, turn, sl 1, rib to end.

Rows 11 & 12: rib 3, *(p1, k1, p1) into next st, rib 5, rep from * 5 times more, rib 1, turn, sl 1, rib to end. 153 [157] sts.

Rows 13 & 14: rib 56, turn, sl 1, rib to end. Cont in same way, working 4 more sts on each alt row until 'rib 96 [100], turn, sl 1, rib to end' has been worked.**

Rib 10 more rows across all sts. Cast off loosely in rib.

Right half: cast on 141 [145] sts and work 1 row of rib starting k1. Work as left half to ** but start row 1 p1 and work increases on row 11 as (k1, p1, k1) into next st. Rib 9 rows across all sts, and cast off in rib.

Waistband: join side and underarm seams using backstitch. Using the smaller needles and A, rs facing, knit up 148 [166] sts along lower edge as follows: 32 [36] sts from each front, 84 [94] sts from back. Work 3½in/9cm in k1, p1 rib. Cast off in rib.

FINISHING

Using backstitch join shoulder and overarm seams. Steam press seams. Neatly oversew centre back seam of collar. Pin collar and bands in position, cast off edges to outside, taking care to match centre back of jacket to centre back of collar, and arrange fullness evenly around collar. Oversew in place from ws. On left front mark position of 3 buttons: 1in/2½cm; 5½in/14cm; 9in/23cm from lower edge. Sew on buttons. Using a medium crochet hook and A, work 3 button loops of 12 chains each along right front edge to correspond with buttons (loops to lay along outer edge). Fasten off securely. Turn in and slip stitch ½in/1cm on each cuff and slip stitch pocket linings in position securely. Do not press.

DOGTOOTH SWEATER

For Tension see Jacket instructions.

SIZES

There are 2 sizes to fit up to 35in/89cm or up to 38in/97cm bust/chest.

Knitted measurements: width at underarm 21½[22½]in/54[56½]cm; length 23[24in]/58½[61]cm; sleeve length 19½in/49½cm.

ABBREVIATIONS

See page 15.

MATERIALS

○ 22 × 25g Mohair in colours as follows:
    12 balls in main colour (A)
    10 balls in contrast colour (B)
○ 2 pairs of needles are required, one pair for st st parts in the size to give correct tension; one pair 2 sizes smaller for ribbing
○ stitch holder

NOTES ON WORKING PATTERN

Ribs: all ribs are worked in k2, p2 twisted rib (i.e. k2, p2 rib with every knit st worked into the back of the stitch).

Note: the first and second sizes are set out separately for back and front.

For additional notes see Jacket instructions.

BACK

Using the smaller needles and A cast on 68[76] sts and work in k2, p2 twisted rib for 2½in/6½cm ending with a rs row.
Change to the larger needles.
Increase row: purl, working twice into 6th [1st] st and every foll alt [3rd] st to last 6 sts [to end]. 97[102] sts.*
First size only:
Row 1(rs): knit 1A, 2B, 2A, 1B, (5A, 2B, 2A, 1B) to last st, 1A.
Row 2(ws): purl 1A, (2B, 2A, 1B, 5A) to last 6 sts, 2B, 2A, 1B, 1A.
Second size only:
Row 1(rs): knit 1B, (5A, 2B, 2A, 1B) to last st, 1A.
Row 2(ws): purl 1A, (2B, 2A, 1B, 5A) to last st, 1B.
Both sizes: cont in patt as set, using chart as a guide until work measures 23[24]in/58½[61]cm from beg, but place markers for armhole after 14[14½]in/35½[37]cm at each side. Knit 1 row B. Cast off loosely, placing markers on 32nd[34th] and 65th[68th] sts for neck.

FRONT

Work as for back to *. Begin patt as follows:
First size only:
Row 1: knit 1B, (5A, 2B, 2A, 1B) to last 6 sts 5A, 1B.
Row 2: purl 1B, 5A, (2B, 2A, 1B, 5A) to last st, 1B.
Second size only: set out patt as for back.
Both sizes: cont in patt as set until work measures 20[20½]in/51[52]cm from beg, ending with a ws row.
Shape neck: patt 40[42] sts, turn and place rem 57[60] sts on stitch holder; cont on these 40[42] sts, and dec 1 st at neck edge of next 8 rows. Work straight until front matches back, cast off loosely. Place sts from st holder back onto needle. With rs facing rejoin yarn, cast off centre 17[18] sts and patt rem 40[42] sts. Cont in patt, dec 1 st at neck edge of next 8 rows. Complete to match first side.

SLEEVES

Using the smaller needles and A cast on 32[36] sts and work in k2, p2 twisted rib for 2in/5cm, ending with a rs row.
Change to the larger needles.
Increase row: purl, working twice into 5th and every foll alt st to last 3[5] sts, purl to end. 45[50] sts.
Begin dogtooth patt as follows:
Row 1(rs): knit first size only (2B, 2A, 1B), both sizes (5A, 2B, 2A, 1B) to end.
Row 2(ws): purl (2B, 2A, 1B, 5A) 4[5] times, first size only, (2B, 2A, 1B).
Shape sleeves: cont in patt, inc 1 st at each end of 5th and every foll 4th row to 83[88] sts, incorporating extra sts into patt. Cont straight in patt until work measures 19½in/49½cm. Cast off.

NECKBAND

Using markers as a guide, join left shoulder seam, using back stitch. With A and smaller needles, rs facing, knit up 34 sts evenly from back neck and 46 sts around front neck edge. 80 sts. Work in k2, p2, twisted rib for 3in/7½cm. Cast off loosely in rib.

FINISHING

Darn in all loose ends. Do not press. Using backstitch join right shoulder seam. Join side and sleeve seams. Set in sleeves. Turn neck band in half to the inside and slip stitch loosely in place, taking care that neckband fits over head.

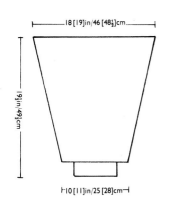

23[24]in/58½[61]cm
9[9½]in/23[24]cm
14[14½]in/35½[37]cm
21½[22½]in/54[56½]cm
18[19]in/46[48½]cm
19½in/49½cm
10[11]in/25[28]cm

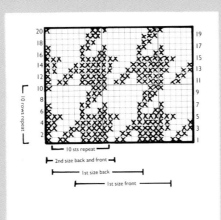

20
18
16
14
12
10
8
6
4
2
19
17
15
13
11
9
7
5
3
1
10 rows repeat
10 sts repeat
2nd size back and front
1st size back
1st size front

TEXTURED TARTAN

These casual sweaters are knitted in a combination of Mohair and Rowan Salad Days Cotton in a multi-coloured 'tartan' pattern. The two yarns are not used together, but alternately, as the intricate-looking pattern is based on slipped stitches. The sleeves are knitted in a one-colour version of the stitch, but could equally well be knitted in the same colours as the body. The styling of one version is fitted, but the alternative version shown is loose and boxy. The collar, waist and edgings are ribbed in mohair.

WAISTED VERSION
SIZES
There are two sizes to fit up to 36in/91cm or up to 40in/102cm bust.
Knitted measurements: width at underarm 21½[24½]in/54½[62]cm; sleeve length 18[18½]in/46[47]cm; length 24½[26]in/62[66]cm approx.

ABBREVIATIONS
See page 15.

MATERIALS
○ 16[17] × 25g balls of Mohair in 3 colours as follows:
    10[11] balls in main colour Black (A)
    3 balls each in colours Gold (B) and Lilac (C)
○ 6 × 50g balls of Rowan Salad Days Cotton in 3 colours as follows:
    2 balls each in colours Black (E) (to match A), Pink (F) and Hyacinth (G)
○ 2 pairs of needles are required, one pair for main parts in the size to give the correct tension; one pair 2 sizes smaller for ribbing.

TENSION
Measured over tartan pattern, 16 sts and 34 rows to 4in/10cm using 5½mm (UK size 5) needles or the size to give correct tension. Recommended needles for edging: 4½mm (UK size 7).

To avoid disappointment, it is essential to check your tension carefully before commencing the garment and use the needles which give **you** the correct tension. **This may not be the size quoted in the standard tension**, as individual knitters vary.

How to check tension: using the recommended needles and A, cast on 26 sts and work 4 rows in garter stitch. Read Notes on working pattern, and cont in pattern as follows:

Rows 1(rs): with E, k1, (yfwd, sl 1, yb, k2) twice; with F, (yfwd, sl 1, yb, k2) twice; with G, (yfwd, sl 1, yb, k2) twice; with E, (yfwd, sl 1, yb, k2) twice, k1 E.

Row 2(ws): k7E, yfwd, k6G, yfwd, k6F, yfwd, k7E.

Row 3: with A, k1, (k2, yfwd, sl 1, yb) rep to last st, k1.

Row 4: knit with A.

Rows 5 to 12: rep rows 1 to 4 twice more.

Rows 13 and 14: rep rows 1 and 2.

Rows 15 and 16: rep rows 3 and 4, **but** using B instead of A.

Rows 17 to 24: rep rows 13 to 16 twice more.

Rows 25 and 26: rep rows 1 and 2.

Rows 27 and 28: rep rows 3 and 4, **but** using C instead of A.

Rows 29 to 36: rep rows 25 to 28 twice more.

With A, work 4 rows in garter st and cast off. Pin the square down flat without stretching. Place a pin between 2 sts near the left, count 16 sts and mark with another pin between the 16th and 17th sts. Mark out 34 rows in the same way. Measure the distance between pins. This should be 4in/10cm in both directions. If it is less your knitting is too tight – try one size larger needle. If it is more, your knitting is too loose – try one size smaller needle. Repeat the process until the correct tension is achieved. Do not be afraid to go up or down more than one needle size. Adjust the size of the second pair of needles accordingly.

As an additional tension check, two vertical bands of pattern (12 sts) measure 3in/7½cm wide; three horizontal bands of patt (36 rows) measure 4½in/10½cm deep. If in doubt, obtain the correct sts tension and work to the lengths given. Note that your tension over the sleeve may not be the same.

NOTES ON WORKING PATTERN
The mohair and cotton yarns are each used for 2 rows alternately, the mohair in horizontal bands one colour at a time, the cotton in vertical bands so all colours are used in each row. Each vertical band of 6 sts is worked using a separate ball of cotton so there are 14[16] balls across the sweater. To minimize tangling, wind several bobbins

24

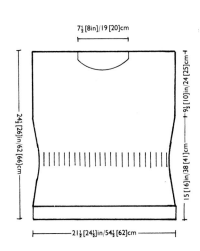

7½ [8in]/19 [20]cm

24½ [26]in/62 [66]cm

9½ [10]in/24 [25]cm

15 [16]in/38 [41]cm

21½ [24½]in/54½ [62]cm

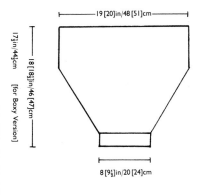

19 [20]in/48 [51]cm

18 [18½]in/46 [47]cm
[for Boxy Version]

17½in/44½cm

8 [9½]in/20 [24]cm

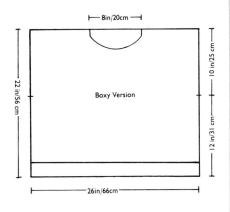

8in/20cm

22 in/56 cm

10 in/25 cm

12 in/31 cm

Boxy Version

26in/66cm

(made from card) of each cotton colour and allow these to hang close to the needle, just unravelling small amounts as needed. When changing cotton colours, ensure you cross yarns on **ws** of work, especially on ws rows, to link colours and prevent holes. All slip sts are slipped purlwise.

BACK

Using the small needles and A, cast on 86 [98] sts.

Rib row 1(rs): p2, (k4, p2), rep to end.
Rib row 2(ws): k2, (p4, k2), rep to end.
Rep 2 rib rows until work measures 2in/5cm, ending with row 2.
Change to the larger needles and joining in colours as required begin patt as follows:
Row 1(rs): with E, k1, *(yfwd, sl 1, yb, k2) twice; with F, (yfwd, sl 1, yb, k2) twice; with G (yfwd, sl 1, yb, k2) twice, rep from * ending with col F [E], k1F [E].
Row 2(ws): k1 F [E], *k6F [E], yfwd, k6E [G], yfwd, k6G [F], rep from * ending with col E, k1E.
Row 3: with A, k1, (k2, yfwd, sl 1, 1, yb) rep to last st, k1.
Row 4: with A, knit.
Rows 5 to 12: rep rows 1 to 4, twice more.
Keeping the cotton colours as now set, repeat the 12 pattern rows, but change the mohair colour (in rows 3 and 4) for each 12 row repeat, using the colours in sequence A, B, C, A, B, C etc. Cont in sequence until work measures approx 8 [9]in/20 [23]cm from beg, ending with a 12th patt row.
Waist rib: change to the smaller needles and A, proceed in rib as follows:
Decrease row(rs): k1 [2], k2tog, (k3, k2tog) rep to last 3 [4] sts, k1 [2], k2tog. 68 [78] sts.
Waist rib row 1 (ws): k0 [2], (p2, k2) to end.
Waist rib row 2 (rs): (p2, k2) rep ending p0 [2].
Rep these 2 rows for 2½in/6cm, ending row 2.

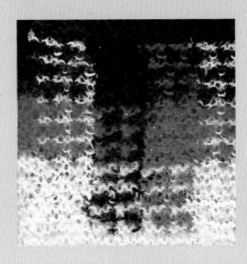

Increase row (ws): purl, working twice into 1st and 3rd [4th] sts, then every foll 4th st to end. 86 [98] sts.

Change to the larger needles, and resume tartan pattern, beg with row 1 and keeping colour sequence correct.

Cont in patt until work measures 15 [16]in/38 [40½]cm from beg. Place a marker for armholes at each end of row. Cont straight in patt until work measures approx 24½ [26]in/62 [66]cm from beg ending with a 12th patt row. Work 1 more row in mohair. Cast off loosely, placing markers on 28th [33rd] and 58th [65th] sts for neck.

FRONT

Work as for back until front measures approx 21½ [23]in/54½ [58]cm, ending with a 12th patt row, rs facing.

Divide for neck: patt 38 [44], turn and leave rem sts on a st holder. Cast off 2 sts at beg (neck edge) of next and foll 2 alt rows. Dec 1 st at neck edge on every foll alt row to 28 [33] sts. Work straight in patt until work matches back to shoulder. Work 1 row in mohair. Cast off loosely. Replace sts from holder onto needle. With rs facing rejoin yarn and cast off centre 10 sts. Cont in patt on rem 38 [44] sts and complete to match first side, reversing shapings.

SLEEVES

Using the smaller needles and A, cast on 32 [38] sts and work in rib as for back for 2in/5cm, ending row 2.

Change to the larger needles and proceed in patt as follows:

Row 1 (rs): with E, k1, (yfwd, sl 1, yb, k2) rep to last st, k1.

Row 2 (ws): with E, knit.

Row 3: with A, sl 1, (k2, yfwd, sl 1, yb) rep to last st, k1.

Row 4: with A, knit.

These 4 rows form the patt, which is worked in A and E only. Cont in patt, but at the same time inc 1 st at both ends of every foll 3rd row to 98 [104] sts, incorporating the extra sts into patt as they occur. Cont with no further shaping until sleeve measures 18 [18½]in/ 46 [47]cm, ending with a 4th patt row. Cast off loosely.

COLLAR

Join left shoulder seam using backstitch.

Using the smaller needles and A, with rs facing, knit up evenly 34 [36] sts from back neck, 40 [42] sts down right front neck, 12 sts from centre front neck, 40 [42] sts up left front neck. 126 [132] sts. Work in rib as follows:

Row 1 (rs): (p1, k4, p1) to end.

Row 2 (ws): (k1, p4, k1) to end.

Rep 2 rib rows until collar measures 4in/10cm.

Cast off loosely in rib using the larger needles.

FINISHING

Do not press. With backstitch seams, join right shoulder. Join sleeves to body using markers as a guide, then join side and sleeve seams. Oversew collar seam, darn in all loose ends.

BOXY VERSION

This version is knitted in a slight variation which uses 1 extra mohair colour. The stripe sequence thus becomes 48 rows in colours A, B, C, D. This variation could also be used in the waisted sweater. This sweater is shorter and wider than the waisted version, and fits all sizes. The collar has been extended to a large polo. Tension and all other details are exactly the same.

MATERIALS

○ 16 × 25g balls of Mohair in 4 colours as follows:

  10 balls in main colour (A), Lilac
  2 balls each in colours (B, C, D), Black, Grey, White

○ 4 × 50g balls of Rowan Salad Days Cotton in 3 colours as follows:

  2 balls in colour (E), Hyacinth
  1 ball each in colours (F, G), Black, White

BACK

Using the smaller needles and A, cast on 104 sts and work as version one (1st size) but omit the waist ribbing and cont straight until back measures approx 22in/56cm, ending with a 12th patt row. Place markers for armholes after 12in/30½cm, and for neck on 37th and 69th sts.

FRONT

Work as back until front measures 19in/48cm from beg, ending with a ws row. Divide for neck as follows: patt 47sts and turn, leave rem sts on a holder. Cast off 2 sts at beg of next and foll 2 alt rows. Dec 1 st at neck edge of every foll alt row to 36 sts. Work straight until front matches back, work 1 row in mohair, cast off. With rs facing, rejoin yarn to sts on holder, cast off centre 10 sts and complete to match first side.

SLEEVES

Work exactly as 2nd size sleeves for version one, but end when sleeve measures 17½in/44½cm.

COLLAR

Work as 2nd size collar for version one, but cont until collar measures 6in/15cm.

FINISHING

As version one.

CURVES

This cardigan can be knitted in either Mohair for a very wearable, everyday cardigan or 100% Angora for evening wear. It is knitted in stocking stitch from the charts and has overlapping curved lines over front, back and sleeves. Both Mohair and Angora soften the lines, but the pattern is just as effective knitted in wool, for example.

SIZES
There are 2 sizes to fit up to 35in/89cm or up to 38in/97cm bust.
Knitted measurements: all round width at underarm 38[41]in/96[104]cm, excluding bands; length 22[23]in/56[58½]cm; sleeve length 22½[23]in/57[58½]cm.

ABBREVIATIONS
See page 15.

MATERIALS
○ 20[21] × 25g balls of Mohair or 20[21] × 20g balls 100% Angora in 5 colours as follows:
   16[17] balls main colour (MC).
   1 ball each of 4 contrast colours, in this mohair cardigan: sea green (SG), mulberry (Mb), blue (Bl) and lilac (Lc)
○ 6 buttons
○ 2 pairs of needles are required, one pair for st st parts in size to give correct tension; one pair 2 sizes smaller for ribbing (3 sizes smaller for Angora version)

TENSION
Measured over st st, 16 sts and 20 rows to 4in/10cm using 5½mm (UK size 5) needles for Mohair version, or 6mm (UK size 4) needles for Angora version. Recommended needles for ribbing: 4½mm (UK size 7).
To avoid disappointment, it is essential to check your tension carefully before commencing the garment and use the needles which give **you** the correct tension. **This may not be the size quoted in the standard tension** as individual knitters vary.
How to check tension: Using the recommended needles and a light colour, cast on 24 sts and work a selected area of pattern from one chart in st st for 30 rows. (See notes on working pattern.) Cast off. Pin the square down flat without stretching. Place a pin between 2 sts near the left, count 16 sts and mark with another pin between the 16th and 17th sts. Mark out 20 rows in the same way. Measure the distance between pins. This should be 4in/10cm in both directions. If it is less your knitting is too tight — try one size larger needle. If it is more, your knitting is too loose — try one size smaller needle. Repeat the process until the correct tension is achieved. Do not be afraid to go up or down more than one needle size. Adjust the size of the second pair of needles accordingly.

NOTES ON WORKING PATTERN

One square of chart represents one stitch. Odd numbered rows are knit (rs) – read from right to left; even numbered rows are purl (ws) – read from left to right. Use a separate ball or length of yarn for each area of colour **including** background colour and avoid stranding yarn across back of work. Cross yarns when changing colour to link colours and prevent gaps appearing in the knitting. To minimize tangling of colours, wind small bobbins (made from card) of each colour and allow them to hang close to the needle, unravelling a small amount at a time as required.

Angora version only: work all ribs in twisted k1, p1 rib by working all knit sts into the **back** of the stitch.

BACK

Using the smaller needles and MC, cast on 69 [74] sts and work in k1, p1 rib for 1in/2½cm.
Increase row: purl, working twice into the first and every foll 10th st. 76 [82] sts. Change to the larger needles. Start working from chart for back at row 1 (bottom right) as follows, joining in colours as appropriate:

Row 1: knit to end.
Row 2: purl to end.
Row 3: knit to end.
Row 4: p61 [64]MC, 1Lc, 14 [17]MC.
Row 5: k14 [17]MC, 1Lc, 61 [64]MC.
Row 6: p54 [57]MC, 1Mb, 6MC, 1Lc, 14 [17]MC.
Cont in patt from chart until row 60 [62] is complete. (Work measures 13 [13½]in/ 33 [34½]cm.)
Shape armholes: cast off 3 sts at beg of next 2 rows and 2 sts at beg of foll 2 rows, Dec 1 st at beg of foll 6 rows. 60 [66] sts. Cont straight

in patt until row 100 [104] is complete. (Back measures 21 [22]in/53½ [56]cm from beg.)
Shape shoulders: cast off 5 sts at beg of next 6 rows and 4 [6] sts at beg of next 2 rows. Cast off rem 22 [24] sts loosely.

FRONTS

Using the smaller needles and MC, cast on 35 [38] sts and work in k1, p1 rib for 1in/2½cm.
Increase row: purl, working twice into every 10th st. 38 [41] sts. Change to the larger needles and start working from appropriate chart at row 1. Cont until row 60 [62] (left) or row 61 [63] (right) is complete.
Shape armhole: cast off 3 sts at beg of next row and 2 sts at beg of foll alt row. Dec 1 st at armhole edge of foll 3 alt rows. 30 [33] sts. Work 3 [1] rows more.
Shape neck: dec 1 st at front edge of next and every foll alt row to 19 [21] sts. Work 7 [9] rows straight, ending at armhole edge.
Shape shoulder: cast off 5 sts at beg of next and foll 2 alt rows. Work 1 row. Cast off rem sts.

SLEEVES

Using the smaller needles and MC, cast on 38 sts and work in k1, p1 rib for 1in/2½cm. Change to the larger needles and start working from chart at row 1 with a knit row, shaping as follows: inc 1 st at each end of the 3rd and every foll alt row, to 52 [54] sts, cont working from chart, then inc 1 st at each end of every foll 12th [10th] row to 60 [64] sts. Work straight until row 72 [74] is complete.
Shape top: cast off 3 sts at beg of next 2 rows. Dec 1 st at each end of every foll 5th row to 44 [48] sts. Dec 1 st at each end of next and every foll row until 28 sts rem. Cast off.
Note: vary colours on second sleeve if you wish.

FRONT EDGINGS AND COLLAR

Knitted throughout in k1, p1 rib using the smaller needles and MC, and worked in one piece starting at bottom edge of right front. (Remember to work twisted rib for Angora version.) Cast on 12 sts and work as follows:

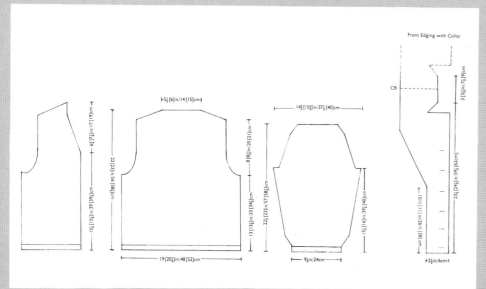

SLEEVES

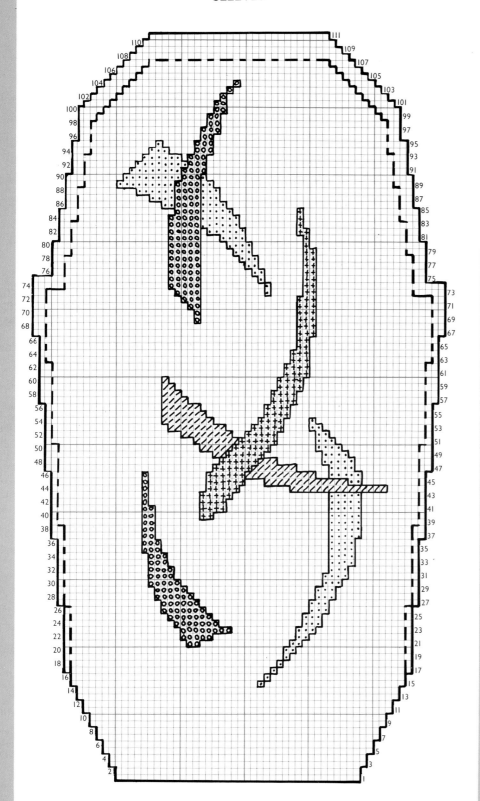

Row 1(rs): sl 1k, p1, (k1, p1) 5 times.
Row 2(ws): (k1, p1) 6 times.
Rep these 2 rows once. Make first buttonhole:
Next row: sl 1k, p1, k1, p2 tog, yrn, rib to end.
Cont straight in rib, slipping first st of rs rows (outer edge) and making 5 more buttonholes at intervals of 2¾in/7cm. At the same time, when work measures 10½[11]in/26½[28]cm, shape **inside** edge only by inc 1 st on next and every foll 3rd row to 25 sts. Mark inside edge with a coloured thread. Cont straight until work measures 21[22]in/53½[56]cm ending with a ws row (at outer edge).
Shape collar: cast off 13 sts at beg of next row. Work 1 row, inc 1 st at beg of next and every foll alt row until there are 18 sts. Cont straight until work measures 26½[28]in/ 67[71]cm from beg, ending with a ws row. Shape second side as reverse of first side, starting as follows: Dec 1 st at beg of next and every foll alt row until 12 sts rem, ending with a ws row. Cast on 13 sts at beg of next row and cont straight until work measures same as first side to coloured marker. Complete to correspond with first side, omitting buttonholes.

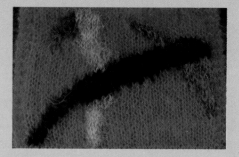

FINISHING

Do not press. Darn in all loose ends carefully, closing up any gaps. Using backstitch, join side and sleeve seams. Set in sleeves making 4 small pleats in the sleeve head to fit into armhole. Pin front band around front and neck edges, aligning points of collar to shoulder seams and buttonholes to right front edge. Oversew in position from the inside. Sew on buttons.

RIGHT FRONT

LEFT FRONT

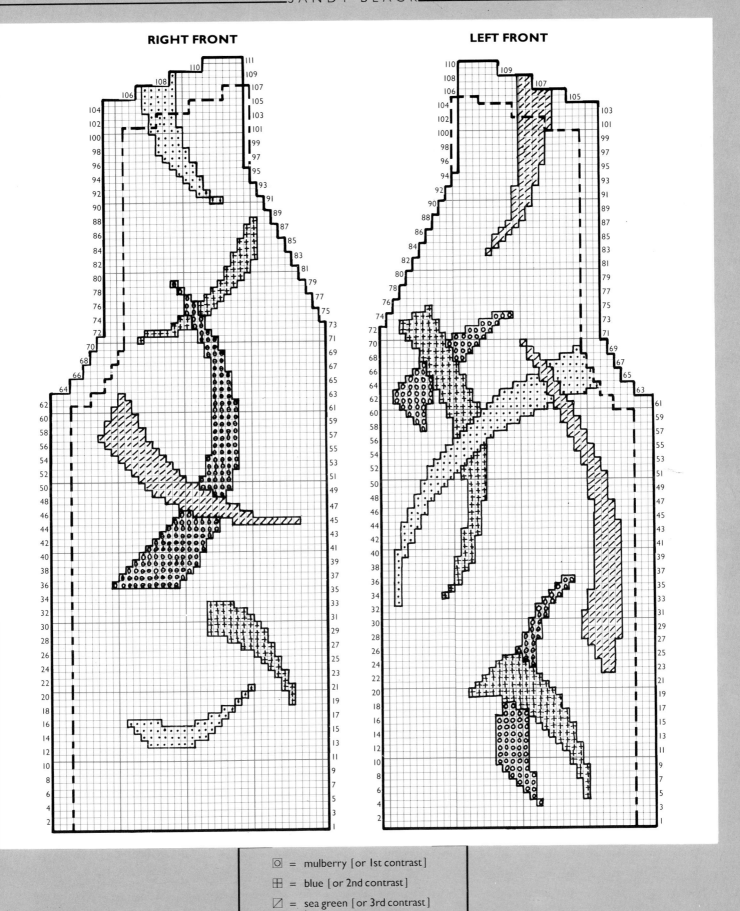

◎ = mulberry [or 1st contrast]

⊞ = blue [or 2nd contrast]

◿ = sea green [or 3rd contrast]

· = lilac [or 4th contrast]

☐ = main colour

- - - - - = 1st size

———— = 2nd size

BACK

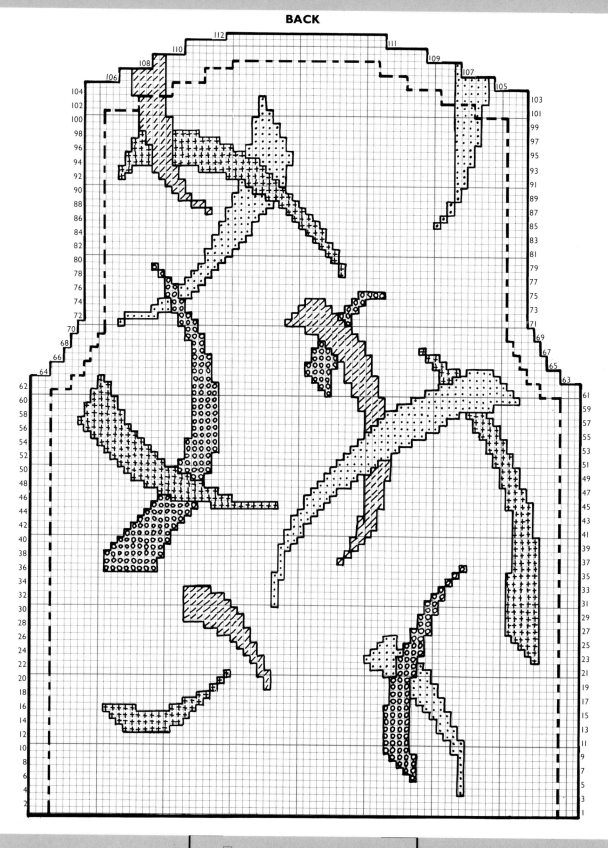

	= mulberry [or 1st contrast]
⊞	= blue [or 2nd contrast]
⊿	= sea green [or 3rd contrast]
⊡	= lilac [or 4th contrast]
☐	= main colour
—·—·—	= 1st size
————	= 2nd size

FAIRISLE FUN SWEATER

The sweater is knitted from the charts using seven colours of Mohair in fairisle bands of stocking stitch with garter stitch ridges in between. The front and back are each knitted in two triangles and sewn together. Ribbed bands and garter stitch ridges are in main colour throughout.

SIZE
One size to fit up to 38in/97cm bust.
Knitted measurements: width at underarm 21in/53cm; length 22in/56cm; sleeve length 20in/51cm.
Note: for a longer sweater, simply knit an extra pattern band (without shaping) on back and front section 1 after the rib has been worked.

ABBREVIATIONS
See page 15.

MATERIALS
○ 24 × 25g balls of Mohair in 7 colours as follows:
  6 balls in main colour (MC)
  3 balls each in 6 contrast colours
Suggested colour combinations: grey or black with
a) pink (Pk), red (Rd), turquoise (Tq), blue (Bl), gold (Gd), fern green (Gn); or
b) pink (Pk), mulberry (Mb), turquoise (Tq), blue (Bl), lilac (Lc), sea green (SG).
○ 2 pairs of needles are required, one pair for main parts in size to give correct tension, one pair 4 sizes smaller for ribbing.

TENSION
Measured over fairisle check patt, 16 sts and 16 rows to 4in/10cm, using 6½mm (UK size 3) needles or the size to give correct tension. Recommended needles for ribbing: 4½mm (UK size 7).
To avoid disappointment, it is essential to check your tension carefully before commencing the garment and use the needles which give **you** the correct tension. **This may not be the size quoted in the standard tension**, as individual knitters vary.
How to check tension: using the recommended needles and 2 colours, A and B, cast on 24 sts and work 24 rows in fairisle check pattern in st st; 2 sts A, 2 sts B for 2 rows, then swop colours for next 2 rows and repeat. Cast off. Pin the square down flat without stretching. Place a pin between 2 sts near the left, count 16 sts and mark with another pin between the 16th and 17th sts. Mark out 16 rows in the same way. Measure the distance between pins. This should be 4in/10cm in both directions. If it is less, your knitting is too tight — try one size larger needle. If it is more, your knitting is too loose

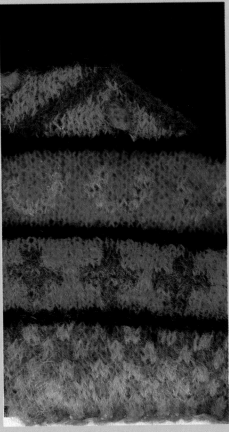

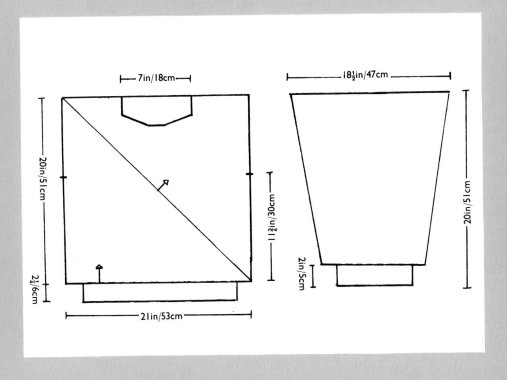

CHART E: RIGHT SLEEVE

1st = Gn or SG
2nd = Pk

1st = Tq
2nd = BL
■ = Rd or Mb

1st = Gd or Lc
2nd = Rd or Mb

1st = Pk
2nd = BL

1st = Rd or Mb
2nd = Tq

1st = Gn or SG
2nd = Gd or LC

1st = Rd or Mb
2nd = BL

1st = Tq
2nd = Pk

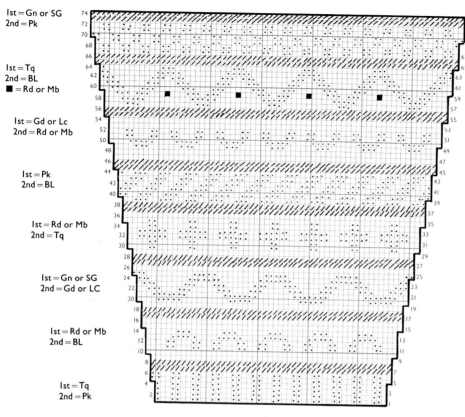

CHART D: LEFT SLEEVE

1st = Gd or LC
2nd = Gn or SG

1st = Pk
2nd = Tq

1st = BL
2nd = Rd or Mb

1st = Gd or LC
2nd = Pk

1st = Tq
2nd = BL

1st = Pk
2nd = Gn or SG

1st = Gd or LC
2nd = Rd or Mb

1st = Pk
2nd = Tq
■ = BL

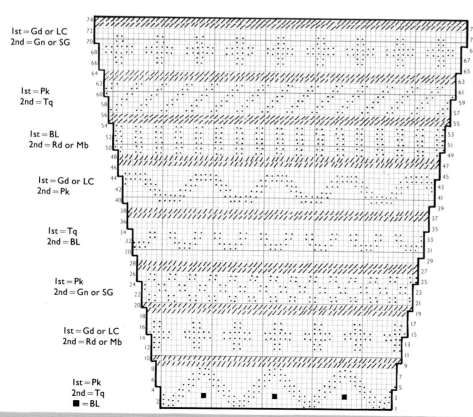

34

– try one size smaller needle. Repeat the process until the correct tension is achieved. Do **not** be afraid to go up or down more than one needle size. Adjust the needle size for ribbing accordingly.

NOTES ON WORKING PATTERN
One square of chart represents one stitch. Odd numbered rows (rs) are knit – read from right to left; even numbered rows (ws) are purl – **except** where marked knit for g st ridges – read from left to right. Ensure that all cast-on and cast-off edges are loose enough to stretch with the knitting. Strand col not in use loosely at the back and weave in evenly every 3rd or 4th st.
Ribs: all ribs are worked in k2, p2 twisted rib, i.e. k2, p2 rib with every knit st worked into the back of the stitch, using needles 4 sizes smaller than for main patt.
Bobbles: where ■ is marked on the chart, make bobble on this st as follows:
With appropriate colour, knit into front and back of next st twice (4 loops). Turn and k4, turn and p4, pass the 3 extra loops over the first, slip bobble st back onto left-hand needle and knit in background colour (abbreviated mb = make bobble).

BACK (section I)
Using the smaller needles and MC, cast on 64 sts and work in k2, p2 twisted rib for 2¼in/5½cm. Change to the larger needles.
Increase row (ws): knit, working twice into the 5th and every foll 3rd st. 84 sts. Starting with row I, commence fairisle patt in cols from chart A, reading odd rows k and even rows p, **except** where marked for garter st ridge between fairisle bands (the g st ridges are in MC throughout). Shape triangle as shown by working 2 sts tog at beg of rs rows and end of ws rows on every row from row 3. Fasten off rem 2 sts.

BACK (section 2)
Using the larger needles and MC, cast on 115 sts (not tightly) and knit 2 rows. Starting with row 3, commence fairisle patt in cols from chart B and dec I st at each end of every row until I st remains and chart is complete. Fasten off. Place markers in a contrast yarn where shown for neck and sleeves.

FRONT (section I)
Work exactly as back section I.

FRONT (section 2)
Working from chart C, work as back section 2 until row 17 of chart is complete.
Divide for neck:
Row 18: p2tog, patt next 6 sts and leave rem sts on holder. Turn.
Row 19: cast off 3 sts, k to last 2 sts, k2tog.
Row 20: sl I, k2tog, psso, fasten off.
With ws facing, return to sts on holder and work from chart as follows:
Shape neck: cast off 11 sts, patt to last 2 sts,

p2tog.
Row 19: k2tog, k to last 2 sts, k2tog.
Row 20: k2tog, k to last 2 sts, k2tog.
Row 21: k2tog, patt to last 2 sts, k2tog.
Cont from chart, dec I st at each end of every row until row 26 is complete, then work without shaping at neck edge until row 35 is complete. 40 sts.
Row 36: inc in first st, patt to last 2 sts, p2tog.
Row 37: k2tog, k to end.
Row 38: inc in first st, k to last 2 sts, k2tog.
Row 39: k2tog, patt to end.
Row 40: inc in first st, patt to last 2 sts, p2tog.
Row 41: k2tog, patt to end.
Cont from chart, dec I st at each end of every row until I st rem and chart is complete. Fasten off.

SLEEVES
Each sleeve is worked from the appropriate chart, D or E, the shaping is identical, but the pattern is different. Using the smaller needles and MC, cast on 32 sts and work in k2, p2 twisted rib for 2in/5cm. Change to the larger needles.
Increase row (ws): knit, working twice into the 5th and every foll alt st. 46 sts. Starting with row I, commence fairisle patt in cols from appropriate chart, inc as shown at each end of every 5th row to 74 sts. When chart is complete, cast off loosely.

FINISHING
Join section I and section 2 of back and front along the diagonal as follows, taking care not to sew too tightly to allow for stretch: slightly overlap section 2 onto section I and backstitch through cast-on edge. Join left shoulder seam with back stitch using markers as a guide.
Neckband: using the smaller needles and MC, rs facing, knit up 28 sts across back neck and 44 sts around front neck edge. 72 sts. Knit I row, then work in k2, p2 twisted rib for 3in/7½cm, cast off very loosely in rib. Darn in all loose ends neatly. Do not press. Join right shoulder seam and neckband. Set in sleeves between markers. Join side and sleeve seams. Turn neckband in half to inside and slip stitch loosely in place, taking care neckband fits over head.

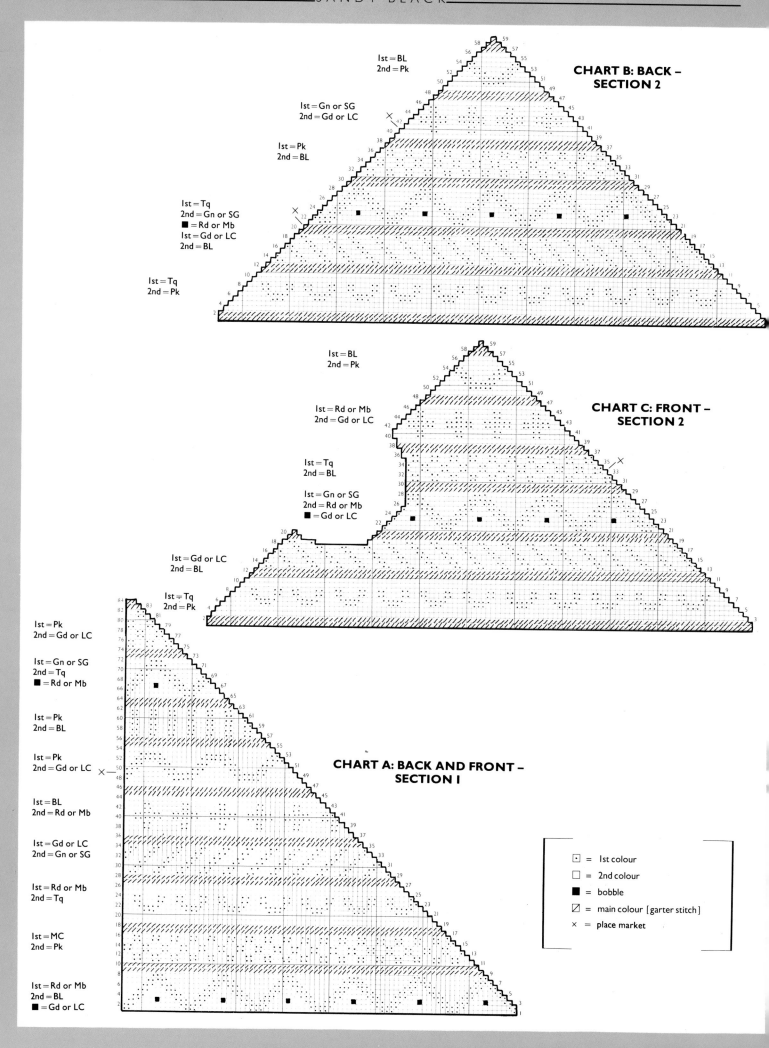

Ist = BL
2nd = Pk

**CHART B: BACK –
SECTION 2**

Ist = Gn or SG
2nd = Gd or LC

Ist = Pk
2nd = BL

Ist = Tq
2nd = Gn or SG
■ = Rd or Mb
Ist = Gd or LC
2nd = BL

Ist = Tq
2nd = Pk

Ist = BL
2nd = Pk

Ist = Rd or Mb
2nd = Gd or LC

**CHART C: FRONT –
SECTION 2**

Ist = Tq
2nd = BL

Ist = Gn or SG
2nd = Rd or Mb
■ = Gd or LC

Ist = Gd or LC
2nd = BL

Ist = Tq
2nd = Pk

Ist = Pk
2nd = Gd or LC

Ist = Gn or SG
2nd = Tq
■ = Rd or Mb

Ist = Pk
2nd = BL

Ist = Pk
2nd = Gd or LC

**CHART A: BACK AND FRONT –
SECTION I**

Ist = BL
2nd = Rd or Mb

Ist = Gd or LC
2nd = Gn or SG

Ist = Rd or Mb
2nd = Tq

Ist = MC
2nd = Pk

Ist = Rd or Mb
2nd = BL
■ = Gd or LC

⊡ = Ist colour

☐ = 2nd colour

■ = bobble

▱ = main colour [garter stitch]

× = place market

36

FAIRISLE FUN CARDIGAN

This summer version of the 'Fairisle Fun' sweater uses the same idea of knitting on the diagonal. It is knitted in Rowan Salad Days Cotton, using six bright, strong colours in the bands of fairisle with black garter stitch ridges in between. Each front is knitted in two triangles, the back in four triangles, which are then sewn together. If you prefer a summer top instead, just sew together the centre front seam. For a different look, try using white or grey as the main colour. If you would like to make it longer, simply repeat a band of pattern before starting the shaping on piece A.

SIZES

There are two sizes to loosely fit up to 36in/91cm or up to 38in/97cm bust.
Knitted measurements: all round width at underarm 44[47]in/112[119]cm; length 19½in/50cm.

ABBREVIATIONS

See page 15.

MATERIALS

○ 12 × 50g balls Rowan 'Salad Days' Cotton in colours as follows:
   3 balls in main colour (MC), Black, Grey, or White
   2 balls each in Jade, Electric Blue, and Pink
   1 ball each in Sunshine, Hyacinth, and Grey
○ 2 pairs of needles are required, 1 pair for main parts in fairisle pattern in the size to give correct tension; one pair 2 sizes smaller for garter stitch edgings
○ 2 buttons
○ medium crochet hook

TENSION

Measured over fairisle pattern 27 sts and 28 rows to 4in/10cm using 4mm (UK size 8) needles, or the size to give the correct tension. Recommended needles for edgings 3¼mm (UK size 10).
To avoid disappointment it is essential to check your tension carefully before commencing the garment and use the needles which give **you** the correct tension. **This may not be the size quoted in the standard tension**, as individual knitters vary.
How to check tension: using the recommended needles and first colour cast on 36 sts. Join in second colour and work 36 rows in fairisle check pattern in st st by rep first 9 rows of chart A 4 times (ignoring all shapings). Cast off loosely. Pin the square down flat without stretching. Place a pin between 2 sts near the left. Count 27 sts and place another pin between 27th and 28th sts. Mark out 28 rows in the same way. Measure

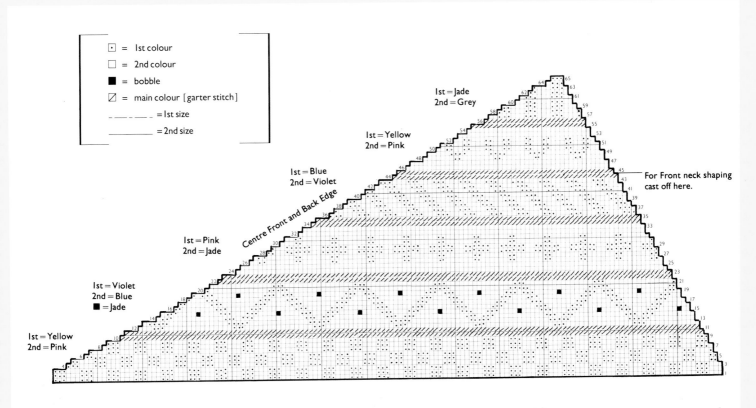

CHART B: BACK AND FRONT DIAGONAL PANELS

37

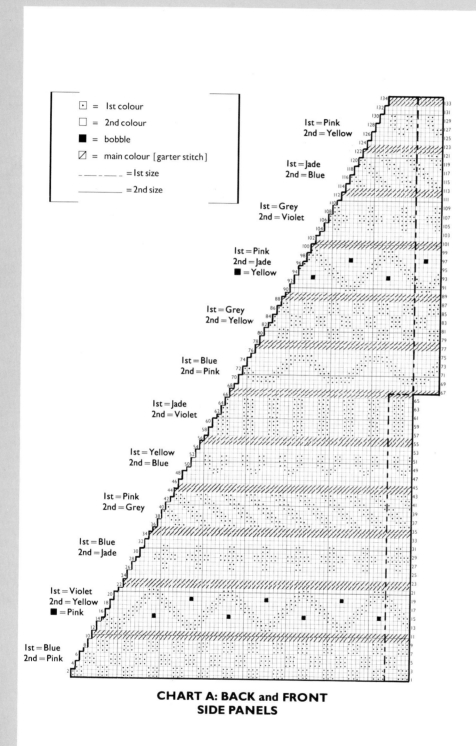

Key:
- ⊡ = 1st colour
- ☐ = 2nd colour
- ■ = bobble
- ▨ = main colour [garter stitch]
- – – – – – = 1st size
- ———— = 2nd size

1st = Pink
2nd = Yellow

1st = Jade
2nd = Blue

1st = Grey
2nd = Violet

1st = Pink
2nd = Jade
■ = Yellow

1st = Grey
2nd = Yellow

1st = Blue
2nd = Pink

1st = Jade
2nd = Violet

1st = Yellow
2nd = Blue

1st = Pink
2nd = Grey

1st = Blue
2nd = Jade

1st = Violet
2nd = Yellow
■ = Pink

1st = Blue
2nd = Pink

**CHART A: BACK and FRONT
SIDE PANELS**

the distance between the pins, this should be 4in/10cm in both directions. If it is less your knitting is too tight – try one size larger needle. If it is more your knitting is too loose – try one size smaller needle. Repeat this process until the correct tension is achieved. Do not be afraid to go up or down more than one needle size. Adjust the size of the needles for edgings accordingly.

NOTES ON WORKING PATTERN
One square of chart represents one stitch. Charts A and B as shown are for **Left Front** and **Right Back** panels only. When working these pieces, odd numbered rows (rs) are knit – read from right to left; even numbered rows (ws) are purl – read from left to right, except for g st ridges.

Right Front and **Left Back** are worked by reversing charts A and B as follows: odd numbered rows (ws) are purl – read from right to left, even numbered rows (rs) are knit – read from left to right, except for g st ridges.

When rs of work is facing, g st ridges between the bands of fairisle are worked by knitting next 2 rows. When ws of work is facing g st ridges are worked by purling next 2 rows.

When working fairisle bands, strand colour not in use loosely at the back, across no more than 3 sts and weave in at intervals.

To follow shaping from the chart: when the outline moves horizontally across one square, this represents a single decrease at the beginning and/or end of the row to be worked next. When the outline moves horizontally across two or more squares, this represents a number of stitches to be cast on or off at the beginning of the numbered row.

Bobbles: Where a solid square is marked on the chart, make a bobble on this st as follows: with appropriate colour knit into the front and back of next st twice (4 loops). (Turn and knit 4, turn and purl 4) twice, pass 1st, 2nd and 3rd sts over 4th st, slip st back onto left-hand needle, and knit this st in background colour. When bobbles occur on ws rows, work as above and push through to rs when complete.

**LEFT FRONT
A: SIDE PANEL**
**Using the smaller needles and MC, cast on 68 [74] sts.
Knit one row and mark ridge with a coloured thread to denote rs of work. Knit a further 4 rows, inc 7 sts evenly across the last row. 75 [81] sts.**
Change to the larger needles and beg working from chart A at row 1 with a k row as follows noting that all odd numbered rows are knit, even numbered rows and purl (see Notes on working pattern), except for g st ridges between pattern bands.
Row 1: knit 3 blue, (3 pink, 3 blue) rep to end.

Row 2: purl 3 blue, (3 pink, 3 blue) rep to end.
Row 3: knit (3 blue, 3 pink) rep to last 3 sts, 1 blue, k2tog using blue.
Cont in this way from chart, dec as shown, and shaping armhole by casting on 6 sts at beg of row 67.

B: DIAGONAL PANEL

Using the smaller needles and MC, cast on 150 sts. Knit 4 rows.
Change to the larger needles and beg working from chart B, at row 1 with a k row as follows, noting all odd numbered rows are knit, even numbered rows are purl, except for g st ridges (see Notes on working pattern).
Row 1: knit (3 pink, 3 yellow) rep to end.
Row 2: purl (3 yellow, 3 pink) rep to end.
Row 3: as row 1.
Row 4: cast off 3 sts, purl 2 yellow (3 pink, 3 yellow) rep to last 6 sts, 3 pink, 1 yellow, p2tog.
Cont in this way shaping the chart, until row 43 has been worked.
Cast off here for front neck.

RIGHT FRONT
A: SIDE PANEL

Work as for Left Front Side Panel from ** to **, then reverse the panel as follows:
Change to the larger needles and beg working from bottom right of chart A at row 1 with a **purl** row, noting that all odd numbered rows are purl – read from left to right; all even numbered rows are knit – read from right to left, except for g st ridges (see Notes on working pattern). Cont as for Left Front Side Panel, in reverse.

B: DIAGONAL PANEL

Work as for Left Front Diagonal Panel, but reversing the panel as above by working all odd numbered rows purl – read from right to left, and all even numbered rows knit – read from left to right, except for g st ridges (see Notes on working pattern).

BACK

Work the 4 panels as given for Left and Right Fronts, **but** when working diagonal panels work until all 65 rows of chart have been completed, so back neck is straight.

FINISHING

Using backstitch seams throughout:
Join back diagonal panels to back side panels, then join these two pieces together at centre back, taking care to match fairisle bands.
Join front diagonal panels to front side panels.
Join shoulder seams on front and back, taking care to match pattern.
Lightly press pieces.
Armhole edgings: using the smaller needles and MC, rs facing, knit up 110 sts evenly along

each armhole edge.
Knit 6 rows. Cast off loosely or use a larger sized needle.
Right front band: using the smaller needles and MC, rs facing, knit up 70 sts from front edge, and 64 sts from front neck edge and round to centre back neck.

Knit 6 rows. Cast off loosely or use a larger sized needle.
Left front band: work to match right front band.
Join side and underarm seams. Join back edging at neck. Using the crochet hook make 2 button loops of crochet chain at top of right front. Fasten off securely, and sew on 2 buttons to correspond. If preferred, more buttons and loops can be added to close the cardigan completely.

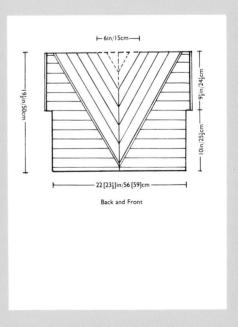

Back and Front

TRIANGLES

The sweater is knitted in Mohair in stocking stitch triangles pattern, and has a ridged yoke and double stand-up collar. Each small triangle is knitted with a separate ball of yarn so beware – at some points there are 17 little balls across the row. The greatest enjoyment in knitting this pattern comes from using the colours entirely at random. Not for the inexperienced.

SIZES
There are 2 sizes to fit up to 35in/89cm or up to 38in/97cm bust.
Knitted measurements: width at underarm 19 [21]in/48 [53½]cm; length 22 [24]in/ 56 [61]cm; sleeve length 18in/46cm.

ABBREVIATIONS
See page 15.

MATERIALS
○ 28 × 25g balls of Mohair in 11 colours as follows:
    8 balls in main colour black, (MC)
    2 balls each of 10 colours for triangles
Many different colour combinations can be devised – if fewer colours are used then more of each colour will be needed
○ 2 pairs of needles are required, one pair for st st parts in the size to give correct tension; one pair 1 size smaller for ribbing
○ 2 stitch holders

TENSION
Measured over triangle patt, 17 sts and 24 rows to 4in/10cm, using 5mm (UK size 6) needles or the size to give correct tension. Recommended needles for ribbing: 4½mm (UK size 7).
To avoid disappointment, it is essential to check your tension carefully before commencing the garment and use the needles which give **you** the correct tension. **This may not be the size quoted in the standard tension,** as individual knitters vary.
How to check tension: using the recommended needles and MC, cast on 25 sts. Using any 6 cols, A, B, C, D, E and F work as follows in st st starting with a k row:
Row 1: knit: 1A, 9B, 1C, 9D, 1E, 4F.
Row 2: purl: 4F, 1E, 9D, 1C, 9B, 1A.
Row 3: 2A, 7B, 3C, 7D, 3E, 3F.
Row 4: 3F, 3E, 7D, 3C, 7B, 2A.
Row 5: 3A, 5B, 5C, 5D, 5E, 2F.
Row 6: 2F, 5E, 5D, 5C, 5B, 3A.
Row 7: 4A, 3B, 7C, 3D, 7E, 1F.
Row 8: 1F, 7E, 3D, 7C, 3B, 4A.
Row 9: 5A, 1B, 9C, 1D, 9E.
Row 10: 9E, 1D, 9C, 1B, 5A.
This corresponds to first 25 sts of chart. Cont from chart, working rows 11–20, then rep rows 1–10, using colours at random. 30 rows. Pin square down flat without stretching. Place a pin between 2 sts near the left, count

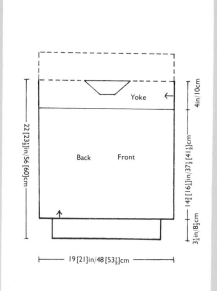

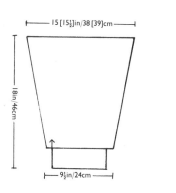

17 sts and place another pin between 17th and 18th sts. Mark out 24 rows in the same way. Measure the distance between pins. This should be 4in/10cm in both directions. If it is less, your knitting is too tight – try one size larger needle. If it is more, your knitting is too loose – try one size smaller needle. Do not be afraid to go up or down more than one needle size. Adjust the needle size for ribbing accordingly.

NOTES ON WORKING PATTERN
One square of chart represents one stitch. Odd numbered rows (rs) are knit – read from right to left; even numbered rows (ws) are purl – read from left to right.
C = contrast colour. All colours are used at random, so this does not refer to any specific colour and **includes main colour.**
Triangle pattern: each triangle is 9 sts at the base, decreasing one st at each side on every alt row to 1 st. Make small butterfly twists (see below) or wind bobbins of all colours and use these at random, leaving ends of about 3in/7cm for finishing off at beg and end of each

triangle. Always cross yarns when changing colour to link colours and avoid holes in the work.
Butterfly twists: measure off yarn in lengths of approx 53in/135cm. Leaving an end hanging in palm of hand, wind yarn in a figure of eight around thumb and little finger, and fasten by wrapping the end of the yarn around the centre a few times and securing with a half knot. Knit from the loose end left at the **beginning** – the yarn does not then unravel during knitting, so minimizing annoying tangling!

BACK
Using the smaller needles and MC, cast on 65 [74] sts.
Row 1(ws): k2, (p1, k2) to end.
Row 2(rs): p2, (k1, p2) to end.
Working in p2, k1 rib as set rib: (4 rows MC, 2 rows C) twice, 6 rows MC, thus ending with a rs row.*
Increase row: purl, inc in 3rd [7th] st and every foll 4th st. 81 [91] sts.

Change to the larger needles. Start working triangles patt, foll chart and joining in 17 [19] twists of colour in random order, including MC:

Row 1: knit 1 st first C, 9 sts second C, 1 st third C, 9 sts fourth C, 1 st fifth C and so on to end of row.

Row 2 and every ws row: purl all sts in the same cols as previous row.

Row 3: knit 2 sts first C, 7 sts second C, 3 sts third C, 7 sts fourth C, 3 sts fifth C, 7 sts sixth C, and so on to end of row.**

Cont working in patt from row 4 of chart until the first 10 rows have been completed (=first band of triangles). Break off all cols. Join in 17 [19] cols in different sequence on next row and work rows 11–20 of chart. Rep the 20 rows of chart, joining in a new col sequence every 10 rows until 90 [100] rows i.e. 9 [10] bands of triangles have been worked.

Make ridge: using MC, work 6 rows in st st ending with a p row. Using a smaller needle, pick up the loops of first row in MC from ws onto this needle. With rs facing, holding the extra needle behind the left-hand needle, knit 1 st from left-hand needle tog with 1 st from the extra needle to end of row. Purl 1 row. Cast off.

FRONT

Work as for back, using the same or a different colour arrangement as preferred.

SLEEVES

Using the smaller needles and MC, cast on 32 sts. Work rib as for back to * but using different cols.

Increase row: purl, working twice into the 6th sts and every foll 3rd st, 41 sts.

Change to the larger needles and work as given for back to ** but using 9 colours

instead of 17 [19]. Cont in triangles patt, inc 1 st at each end of every 6th [5th] row, incorporating the extra sts into patt, until there are 65 [67] sts. Work straight until 9 bands of triangles have been worked (90 rows). Cast off using all cols in turn.

Work the second sleeve in the same way, using the same or a different colour arrangement as preferred.

YOKE

Using the larger needles and MC, cast on 34 sts and work 8 rows in st st, starting with a knit row. Make the first ridge by picking up loops from **2nd** row in MC and knitting tog with sts on needle.* Join in any C and work 5 rows in st st, break off C. Using MC, work 6 rows in st st and make ridge as given for back. Repeat from * 4 [5] times more, using a different C each time. 6 [7] ridges in MC.

Divide for neck: with next C, purl 17 sts and leave on a st holder. Cont straight in ridge patt as before on rem 17 sts for back neck until a further 5 ridges and 6 coloured stripes have been worked, leave on a st holder. With rs facing, replace 17 sts for front neck onto needle and rejoin yarn to inside edge.

Shape front neck: cast off 4 sts at beg of next row, and cont in ridge patt but dec 1 st at neck edge on 3rd, 4th and 5th rows of first C stripe, and 2nd, 3rd and 4th rows of next stripe in C. 7 sts rem. Cont straight in ridge patt until 4th ridge after dividing for neck is complete. Cont in patt, inc 1 st at neck edge on 2nd, 3rd, and 4th rows of next stripe in C, and 1st, 2nd and 3rd rows of foll stripe. Cast on 4 sts at neck edge on next row and complete to match back neck. 17 sts. Break yarn. Replace 17 sts from back neck onto needle. Rejoining back and front, cont in ridge patt until 6 [7] more ridges have been completed. 17 [19] ridges from beg. Cast off.

COLLAR

Using the smaller needles and MC, loosely cast on 77 sts and working in p2, k1 rib as for back, rib: (4 rows MC, 1 row C) 4 times, 6 rows MC, (1 row C, 4 rows MC) 4 times. Rib 1 row C and cast off loosely. Oversew cast off and cast on edges of collar together loosely.

FINISHING

Do not press. Darn in all loose ends carefully, closing up gaps between colours at the same time. Taking care to preserve ridges at seams, and using backstitch, join yoke to front and back. Join sleeves to straight edge of body and yoke, taking care to match centre of sleeves to centre of yoke. Join side and sleeve seams. With oversewn edge to neck edge and rs together, pin collar in position all round neck, taking care to position the opening exactly at centre front. Sew in place and oversew open ends of collar. Take care that opening fits over head.

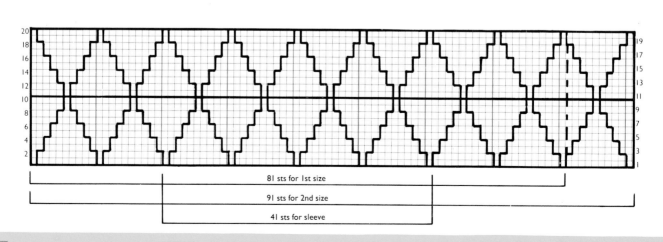

81 sts for 1st size

91 sts for 2nd size

41 sts for sleeve

_ _ _ _ _ _ _ _ = 1st size

_____ = 2nd size

FANS

I have decorated this simple boxy-shaped cardigan with colourful fan motifs scattered over the whole shape. The cardigan is knitted in Mohair in stocking stitch from the charts and has fan motifs on the back, front and sleeves with embroidered 'tails'.

SIZES
There are 2 sizes to fit up to 36in/92cm or up to 38in/97cm bust.
Knitted measurements: all round width at underarm 40½ [43½]in/103 [110]cm, including front bands; length 22½ [23½]in/57 [59]cm; sleeve length 22½ [23½]in/57 [59]cm.

ABBREVIATIONS
See page 15.

MATERIALS
○ 21 × 25g balls of Mohair in 6 colours as follows:
    16 balls in main colour (MC)
    1 ball each in 5 contrast colours, in this example: sea green, red, pink, blue and gold
○ 4 large buttons
○ 2 pairs of needles are required, one pair for st st parts in size to give the correct tension; one pair 2 sizes smaller for ribbing
○ stitch holder
○ large-eyed yarn needle
○ medium crochet hook

TENSION
Measured over st st, 16 sts and 20 rows to 4in/10cm using 5½mm (UK size 5) needles, or the size to give correct tension. Recommended needles for ribbing: 4½mm (UK size 7).
To avoid disappointment, it is essential to check your tension carefully before commencing the garment and use the needles which give **you** the correct tension. **This may not be the size quoted in the standard tension**, as individual knitters vary.
How to check tension: using the recommended needles and MC, cast on 24 sts and work first fan motif from chart for right front (see notes on working pattern) as follows: work from sts 10 to 34 on knit rows and sts 34 to 10 on purl rows, for 30 rows in all. Cast off. Pin the square down flat without stretching. Place a pin between 2 sts near the left, count 16 sts and mark with another pin between the 16th and 17th sts. Mark out 20 rows in the same way. Measure the distance between pins. This should be 4in/10cm in both directions. If it is less your knitting is too tight – try one size larger needle. If it is more, your knitting is too loose – try one size smaller needle. Repeat the process until the correct tension is achieved. Do not be afraid to go up or down more than one needle size.

Adjust the size of the second pair of needles accordingly.

NOTES ON WORKING PATTERN
One square of chart represents one stitch. Odd numbered rows (rs) are knit – read from right to left; even numbered rows (ws) are purl – read from left to right. Use a separate ball or length of yarn for each area of colour, **including** background colour and avoid stranding yarn across back of work. Cross the yarns when changing colour to link the colours and prevent gaps appearing in the knitting. To minimize tangling of colours, wind small bobbins (which can be made from card) of each colour and allow them to hang close to the needle, unravelling a small amount at a time as required.

BACK
Using the smaller needles and MC, cast on 71 [76] sts and work in k1, p1 rib for 1in/2½cm.
Increase row: purl, working twice into 3rd and every following 10th st, 78 [84] sts. Change to the larger needles and st st and starting with a knit row work from chart for back from row 1. Cont in patt from chart until row 60 [62] is complete.

Shape armholes: cast off 3 sts at beg of next 2 rows, 2 sts at beg of foll 2 rows. Dec 1 st at beg of next 6 rows. 62 [68] sts. Cont straight until row 100 [104] is complete. (Back measures 21 [22]in/53 [56]cm from beg.)
Shape shoulders: cast off 5 sts at beg of next 6 rows and 4 [5] sts at beg of next 2 rows. Leave rem 24 [28] sts on holder for neckband.

RIGHT FRONT
Pocket lining: using the larger needles and MC, cast on 21 sts and work in st st for 9in/23cm. Leave on a st holder or spare needle.
Using the smaller needles and MC, cast on 35 [38] sts and work in k1, p1 rib for 1in/2½cm.
Increase row: purl, working twice into every 10th st. 38 [41] sts. Change to the larger needles. Start working from chart for right front at row 1 and cont until row 30 is complete. Cont in MC as follows:*
Row 31 (rs): k10, rib 21, k to end.
Row 32: p7 [10], rib 21, p to end.
Row 33: k10, rib 21, k to end.
Repeat last 2 rows once more.
Divide for pocket: p7 [10], cast off next 21 sts ribwise, slip last st back onto left-hand needle, break yarn. With ws facing, rejoin MC and p21 sts from pocket lining, p10. Note

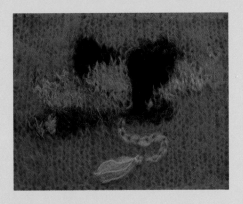

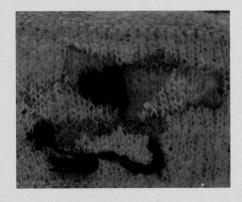

BACK

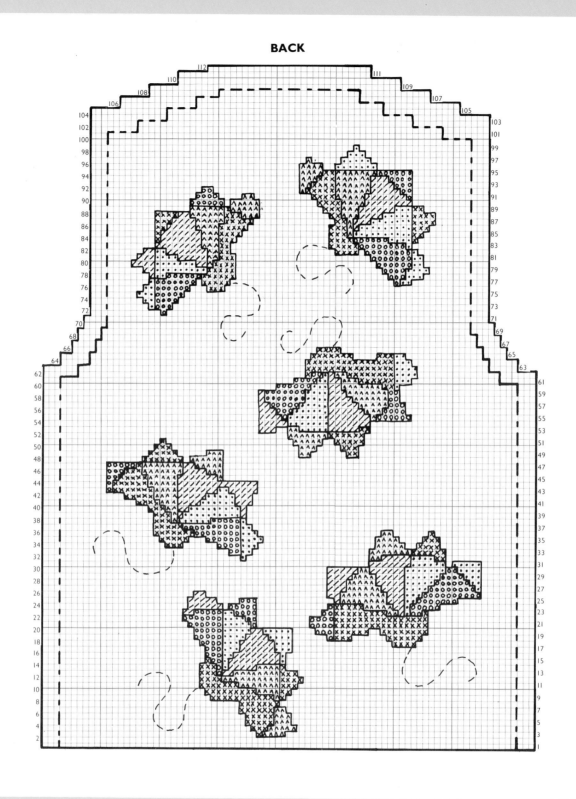

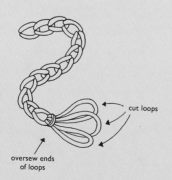

cut loops

oversew ends
of loops

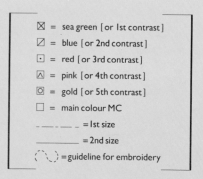

⊠ = sea green [or 1st contrast]

⊿ = blue [or 2nd contrast]

⊡ = red [or 3rd contrast]

⊿ = pink [or 4th contrast]

⊙ = gold [or 5th contrast]

☐ = main colour MC

– – – = 1st size

——— = 2nd size

⌒⌒ = guideline for embroidery

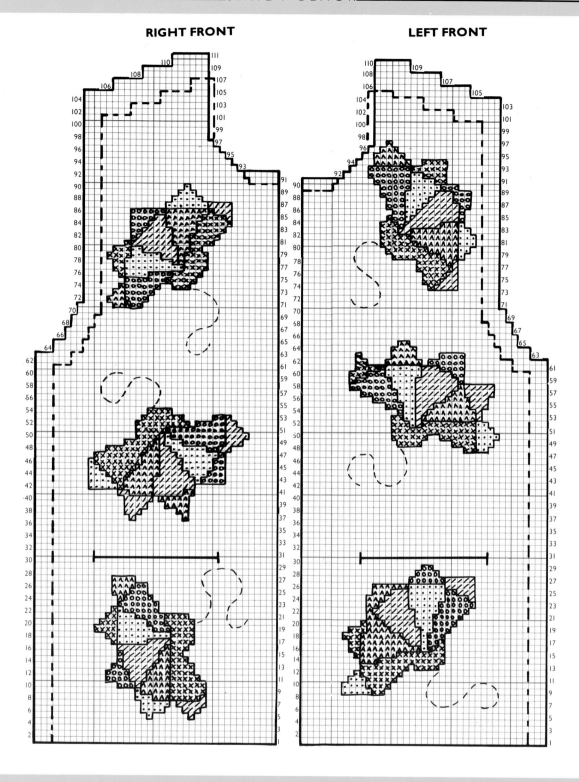

RIGHT FRONT   LEFT FRONT

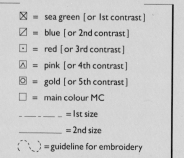

⊠ = sea green [or 1st contrast]

⊡ = blue [or 2nd contrast]

⊡ = red [or 3rd contrast]

⊿ = pink [or 4th contrast]

⊙ = gold [or 5th contrast]

□ = main colour MC

— ·— ·— = 1st size

————— = 2nd size

(͡) = guideline for embroidery

pocket lining will be doubled. ** Cont straight in patt from chart until row 61 [63] is complete.

Shape armhole: cast off 3 sts at beg of next row and 2 sts at beg of foll alt row. Dec 1 st at side edge of foll 3 alt rows. 30 [33] sts. Cont until row 90 [92] is complete.

Shape neck: cast off 5 [7] sts at beg of next row. Dec 1 st at neck edge of foll 6 [5] rows. 19 [21] sts. Work 4 [7] rows more.

Shape shoulder: cast off 5 sts at beg of next and foll 2 alt rows. Work 1 row. Cast off rem sts.

SLEEVES

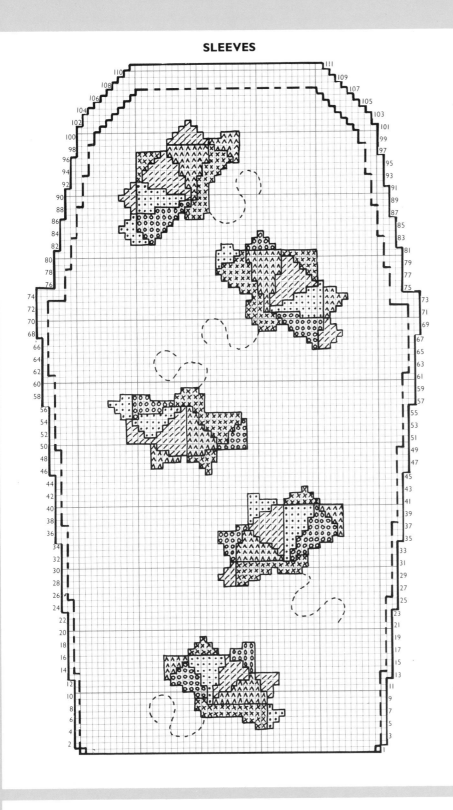

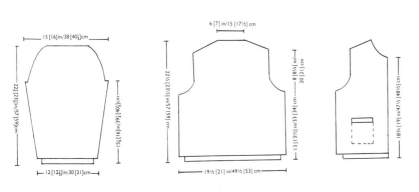

LEFT FRONT
Work as for right front to *.

Row 31: k7 [10], rib 21, k10.

Row 32: p10, rib 21, p7 [10].

Row 33: k7 [10], rib 21, k10.

Repeat last 2 rows once more.

Divide for pocket: p10, cast off next 21 sts ribwise, slip last st back onto left-hand needle, break yarn. With ws facing, rejoin MC and p21 sts from pocket lining, p7 [10]. Cont as for right front from **, but reverse shapings by working one less row before shapings.

SLEEVES
Using the smaller needles and MC, cast on 36 [38] sts and work in k1, p1, rib for 1in/2½cm.

Increase row: purl, working twice into every 3rd st. 48 [50] sts. Change to the larger needles and starting with a knit row work from chart for sleeve from row 1. Inc 1 st at each end of 2nd and every foll 12th [11th] row to 60 [64] sts. Work straight until row 72 [74] is complete. (Sleeve measures 15½ [16]in/39½ [40]cm from beg.)

Shape top: cast off 3 sts at beg of next 2 rows. Dec 1 st at each end of the foll 5th [6th] row and every foll 5th row to 44 [48] sts. Work 1 row. Dec 1 st at each end of next and every foll row to 30 [32] sts. Cast off.

FRONT BANDS
Using the smaller needles and MC, cast on 12 sts and work in k1, p1 rib until band fits up front edge. Cast off in rib. (Make two.)

COLLAR
Join shoulder seams using backstitch. With rs facing, using the smaller needles and MC, knit up 23 [24] sts from right front neck, 24 [28] sts from back neck, 23 [24] sts from left front neck. 70 [76] sts. Work in k1, p1 rib for 4in/10cm, cast off loosely in rib.

FINISHING
Do not press. Sew in all loose ends.

To embroider tails: use lengths of leftover yarn approx 36in/91cm long. Taking the dotted lines on the chart as a guide, and using chain st, embroider a tail on each fan. When you have worked the last chain, do not break yarn, but work tassel with rest of thread as follows: * wrap yarn around 2 fingers once and catch yarn down through the last chain. Repeat from * twice more (3 loops). Oversew the end of the loops where they join the chain st. Secure end. Cut loops (see diagram).

Oversew front bands in place. Fold up pocket linings and stitch in position to base of pocket bands. Sew pocket sides. Using backstitch, join side and sleeve seams. Set in sleeves, making 4 pleats at sleeve head facing away from shoulder seams.

On left front, mark position of 4 buttons with pins, spacing them evenly along the front band. Sew on buttons. Using a medium crochet hook and MC, work 4 button loops of 12 chain along right front edge to correspond with buttons (see diagram), and fasten off securely.

47

RECTANGLES

This design is relatively easy for anyone who has not worked from charts. The sweater is knitted in Mohair in stocking stitch from the charts, using 6 colours. The ribbed bands and collar are knitted in random stripes. Colours given are for the bright colourway but have fun devising your own colour combinations.

SIZES
There are 2 sizes to fit up to 35in/89cm or up to 38in/97cm bust loosely.
Knitting measurements: width at underarm 20 [21½]in/51 [55]cm; length 23 [24]in/58½ [61]cm; sleeve length 20½in/52cm with cuff turned back.

ABBREVIATIONS
See page 15.

MATERIALS
○ 20 × 25g balls of Mohair in 6 colours as follows:
   3 balls each in red (Rd), green (Gn), gold (Gd) and pink (Pk)
   4 balls each in turquoise (Tq) and blue (Bl) to knit either size sweater
○ 2 pairs of needles are required, one pair for st st parts in the size to give correct tension; one pair 2 sizes smaller for ribbing
○ Optional: circular needle or set of 4 double-pointed needles in smaller size

TENSION
Measured over st st, 16 sts and 20 rows to 4in/10cm, using 5½mm (UK size 5) needles or the size to give the correct tension. Recommended needles for ribbing: 4½mm (UK size 7).
To avoid disappointment, it is essential to check your tension carefully before commencing the garment and use the needles which give **you** the correct tension. **This may not be the size quoted in the standard tension** as individual knitters vary.
How to check tension: using the recommended needles and a light colour, cast on 24 sts and work in st st for 30 rows. Cast off. Pin the square down flat without stretching. Place a pin between 2 sts near the left, count 16 sts and mark with another pin between the 16th and 17th sts. Mark out 20 rows in the same way. Measure the distance between the pins. This should be 4in/10cm in both directions. If it is less, your knitting is too tight – try one size larger needle. If it is more, your knitting is too loose – try one size smaller needle. Do not be afraid to go up or down more than one needle size and adjust the size of the second pair of needles accordingly.

SLEEVES

Blues colourway

Bl	=	royal blue
Gn	=	sea green
Tq	=	turquoise
Rd	=	mulberry
Gd	=	lilac
Pk	=	teal blue

Bright colourway

Bl	=	saxe blue
Gn	=	fern green
Tq	=	turquoise
Rd	=	red
Gd	=	gold
Pk	=	pink
– – – – –	=	1st size
———	=	2nd size

NOTES ON WORKING PATTERN

One square of chart represents one stitch. Odd numbered rows (rs) are knit – read from right to left; even numbered rows (ws) are purl – read from left to right. Use a separate ball or length of yarn for each area of colour, and cross the yarns when changing colour to link the colours and prevent holes. To minimize tangling of colours, wind small bobbins (which can be made from card) of each colour, and allow these to hang close to the needle, unravelling a small amount at a time as required.

BACK

Using the smaller needles and first col for waistband, cast on 60 [64] sts and work in k2, p2 twisted rib (i.e. with every knit st worked into the back of the stitch) for 2½in/6½cm changing col every 2 rows and using all cols at random. Break yarn after each stripe, except last col.

Increase row: purl, working twice into first and every foll 3rd st, thus inc to 80 [86] sts. Change to the larger needles. Join in cols and start working patt from chart at row 1 as follows:

Row 1: knit 9 [12]Gn, 15Rd, 14Bl, 27Gd, 15 [18]Bl.

Row 2: purl 15 [18]Bl, 27Gd, 14Bl, 15Rd, 9 [12]Gn.

Repeat these two rows once and first row once more. Join in Pk on next row as follows:

Row 6: purl 11 [14]Bl, 17Pk, 14Gd, 14Bl, 15Rd, 9 [12]Gn.

Row 7: knit 9 [12]Gn, 15Rd, 14Bl, 14Gd, 17Pk, 11 [14]Bl.

Cont in patt, following cols from chart until row 52 [56] is complete. (Work measures 12¾ [13½]in/32½ [34]cm from beg.)

Shape armholes: cast off 9 [10] sts at beg of next 2 rows**. Cont in patt without shaping until row 96 [102] is complete. (Work measures 21½ [22¾]in/54½ [57½]cm from beg.)

Shape shoulders: cast off 6 [7] sts at beg of next 4 rows. Cast off 6 sts at beg of next 2 rows. Cast off rem 26 sts.

FRONT

Work as for back to **. Cont in patt without shaping until row 84 [88] of chart is complete, thus ending with rs facing for next row.

Divide for neck: patt 26 [28] sts and turn, leave rem sts on a st holder. Cont on these 26 [28] sts for first side as follows:

Shape neck: working from right half of chart, dec 1 st at neck edge of next 8 rows. 18 [20] sts. Cont straight in patt on these sts until row 96 [102] is complete.

Shape shoulder: case off 6 [7] sts at beg of next and foll alt row. Work 1 row. Cast off rem sts.

Second side: return to sts on holder, with rs facing, cast off centre 10 sts and cont on rem sts. Shape to correspond with first side, but follow patt from left half of chart, and work 1

extra row before shoulder shaping.

SLEEVES

Using the smaller needles and first col for cuff, cast on 32 [34] sts and work in striped k2, p2 twisted rib as before for 4in/10cm. Do not break off last col.

Increase row: purl, working twice into the 3rd [5th] st and every foll 3rd st. 42 [44]sts. Change to the larger needles. Join in cols for first row of sleeve chart as follows:

Row 1: knit 14 [15]Tq, 23Gn, 5 [6]Gd.

Row 2: purl 5 [6]Gd, 23Gn, 14 [15]Tq.

Cont in patt from chart, inc 1 st at each end of the 6th [5th] row and every foll 6th [5th] row until there are 68 [72] sts. Work straight until chart is complete. (Sleeve measures 22½in/57cm from beg.) Cast off using each col in turn.

Work second sleeve exactly as first, but work a different colour arrangement in the cuff.

COLLAR

Using the smaller needles and first col, loosely cast on 84 [88] sts and work in striped twisted k2, p2 rib as before for 5in/12½cm, changing col every 3 rows and using cols at random. Cast off loosely in rib.

Alternative method: join shoulder seams using backstitch. Using a circular needle or set of 4 needles, with rs facing, knit up 84 [88] sts around neck edge, starting and finishing at centre front. Work in rows back and forth, changing col every 3 rows. Cast off loosely in rib.

FINISHING

Do not press. Darn in loose ends carefully, closing up all gaps. Using backstitch seams, join shoulders, if necessary. Set sleeves squarely into armholes, fitting the corner of the sleeve squarely into the right angle of the armhole shaping. Join the first part of each side of sleeve to cast-off sts at underarm. Join rest of sleeve seam and side seams. Neaten cuffs and waistband. Fold back cuffs.

Collar: With rs tog and cast-off edge of collar to neck edge, pin collar around neck, starting and finishing at the centre front. Oversew neatly in place. Sew tog first 3 stripes of front opening and then turn a narrow hem on each edge to neaten.

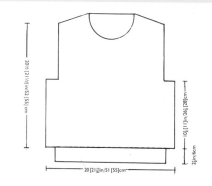

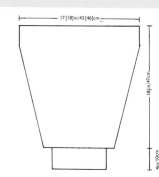

BACK AND FRONT

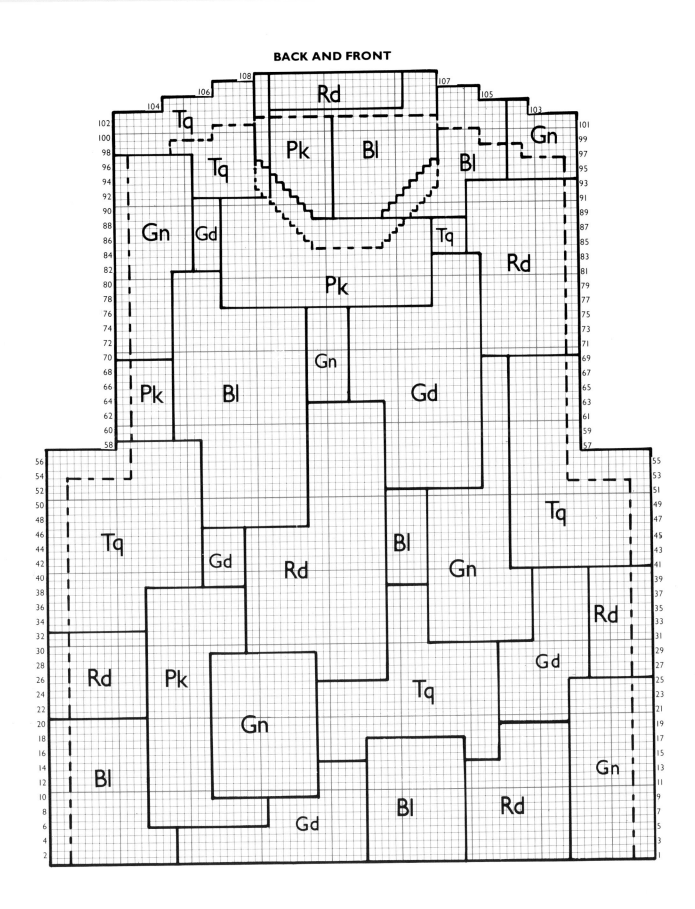

which give **you** the correct tension. **This may not be the size quoted in the standard tension**, as individual knitters vary.

How to check tension: using the recommended needles and S, cast on 36 sts and purl 1 row. Join in C and work as follows in st st, crossing colours where they meet (see Notes on working pattern):
Row 1: knit 16S, 20C. **Row 2:** purl 20C, 16S.
Row 3: knit 17S, 19C. **Row 4:** purl 19C, 17S.
Row 5: knit 18S, 18C. **Row 6:** purl 18C, 18S.
Row 7: knit 19S, 17C. **Row 8:** purl 17C, 19S.
Row 9: knit 20S, 16C. **Row 10:** purl 16C, 20S.
Row 11: knit 21S, 15C.
Now work in reverse order rows 10 to 1. Repeat the whole sequence from row 2. 41 rows. Cast off. Pin the square down flat without stretching. Place a pin between 2 sts near the left, count 22 sts and mark with another pin between the 22nd and 23rd st. Mark out 27 rows in the same way. Measure the distance between pins. This should be 4in/10cm in both directions. If it is less your knitting is too tight — try one size larger needle. If it is more, your knitting is too loose — try one size smaller needle. Repeat the process until the correct tension is achieved. Adjust the size of the second pair of needles accordingly.

NOTES ON WORKING PATTERN

One square of chart represents one stitch. Odd numbered rows (rs) are knit – read from right to left; even numbered rows (ws) are purl – read from left to right. Use a separate ball or length of yarn for each separate area of colour. Cross yarns when changing colour to link the colours and prevent holes appearing in the knitting. For best results avoid any stranding of yarns at the back. To minimize tangling, wind bobbins (which can be made from card) of each colour and allow these to hang close to the needle, just unravelling small amounts as required.

To follow shaping from the chart: where the outline moves out by one square this represents a single increase in the first or last st of the row to be worked next.

BACK AND FRONT

Using the smaller needles and S, cast on 100 [108] sts, and work in st st for 1in/2½cm, ending with a knit row. Knit 1 row to make a ridge for lower hem edge.

Change to the larger needles and beg working from chart at row 1, with a knit row as follows, using a separate ball for each colour group (9 in first row):
Row 1(rs): knit 4[8]S, 11M, 12S, 19N, 12S, 19M, 8S, 11M, 4[8]S.
Row 2: purl 5[9]S, 9M, 10S, 17M, 14S, 17N, 14S, 9M, 5[9]S.
Row 3: knit 0[1]N, 6[9]S, 7M, 16S, 15N, 16S,

MATISSE

This extrovert summer dress was inspired by the colourful paper cut outs of Matisse. It is knitted in Rowan 'Salad Days' Cotton in stocking stitch from a chart, using a vivid combination of six strong colours.

SIZES

There are two sizes to fit up to 36in/91cm or up to 38in/97cm hips.

Knitted measurements: length including straps 35in/89cm; width at underarm 21 [22½]in/53½ [57]cm.

ABBREVIATIONS

See page 15.

MATERIALS

52 ○ 13 × 50g balls of Rowan Salad Days Cotton in

6 colours as follows:
   3 balls in Sunshine (S)
   2 balls each of Copper (C), Bright Pink (P), Hyacinth (H), Moss (M), and Marine (N)
○ 3 pairs of needles are required, 2 pairs for body and facings in the size to give the correct tension; one pair 2 sizes smaller for edgings.
○ 4 buttons

TENSION

Measured over stocking stitch pattern 22 sts and 27 rows to 4in/10cm using 4mm (UK size 8) needles or the size to give correct tension. Recommended needles for edgings: 3¼mm (UK size 10).

To avoid disappointment, it is essential to check your tension carefully before commencing the garment and use the needles

15M, 12S, 7M, 6 [9]S, 0 [1]N.
Cont in this way from chart, inc 1 st at both ends of 21st and every foll 15th row, as shown on chart, until there are 116 [124] sts. Cont working straight from chart until row 150 is complete, then cont in patt, but inc 1 st at both ends of next and every foll 3rd row until there are 130 [138] sts, then inc 1 st at both ends of foll 3 rows. Cast on 2 sts at beg of next 2 rows. 140 [148] sts. Cont from chart with no further shaping until row 216 is complete. Leave sts on a spare needle.

BACK AND FRONT FACINGS

Using the larger needles and S, cast on 140 [148] sts, and work in st st for 3in/7½cm, ending with a k row. Leave sts on needle and return to sts for back or front. Join facing to body of dress, and position shoulder straps, by casting off sts from both pieces together as follows:
With both sets of sts on needles, place ws together with rs of body towards you. Using M knit together first st of body with first st of facing; rep for 2nd stitch, cast off first st. Cont in this way, changing colours to match pattern as necessary, but leave 4 sets of 6 sts each from body and facing on lengths of yarn for straps as shown on chart. (To avoid breaking a colour, knit across sts for top of straps before leaving them on yarn.)

SHOULDER STRAPS

Front: return to sts of dress front held on yarn, and using matching colours work, 6in/15cm in st st on each group of 6 sts for top of straps. Leave sts on a length of yarn.
Facing: with S, knit 6in/15cm in st st on each group of 6 sts from front facing, leave sts on length of yarn.

FINISHING AND ARMBANDS

Carefully darn in all loose ends, closing any gaps in the work. Using backstitch seam join side seams.
Left and right armbands: using the smaller needles, rs facing and beg at top cast off edge, knit up 40 sts with N, then 40 sts with M. 80 sts. Work in k1, p1 rib in colours as set for 4in/10cm, crossing yarns on ws when changing colour to link tog. Cast off in colours in rib.
Fold armbands in half onto ws and slip stitch in position catching facings into seams at the same time. Slip stitch facings to inside of front and back. Oversew open ends of armbands together using matching colour. Pin shoulder straps in position on back and graft each side to back and facing separately. Oversew strap facings to straps. Fold lower hem edge up onto ws along marker row and slip stitch in position. Join armbands together at top outer corner by sewing on 2 buttons, one on each side, at the same time.

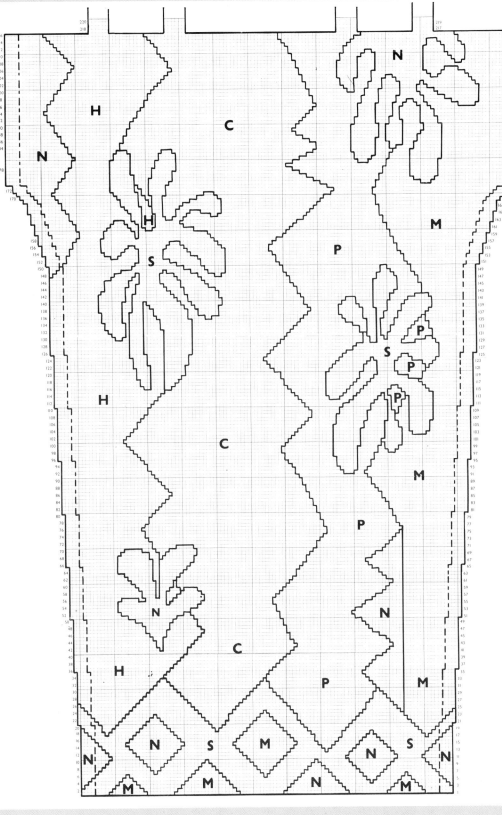

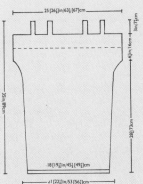

S = sunshine
P = pink
N = marine
M = moss green
C = copper
H = hyacinth

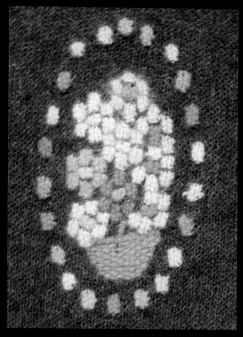

section 2
FLORAL

THERE IS HARDLY ANYTHING MORE APPEAL-
ING THAN A BOUQUET OF FRESH FLOWERS
ARRANGED IN A PLEASING VASE, ESPECIALLY
FOR ANYONE LIKE MYSELF WITHOUT A GARDEN.
GLADIOLI, TULIPS, ANEMONES, IRISES AND, OF
COURSE, ROSES ARE ALL FAVOURITES OF MINE,
AND HAVE ALL APPEARED IN MY KNITWEAR,
SOMETIMES ELEGANTLY ALONE, SOMETIMES IN
PROFUSE ABUNDANCE. I HAVE USED THEM
IN EVERYTHING FROM PRETTY CARDIGANS,
AND STRIKING EVENING WEAR TO CASUAL
SWEATERS. I CHOSE ANGORA OR MOHAIR FOR
MOST OF THE DESIGNS ON THE FOLLOWING
PAGES, PARTICULARLY BECAUSE OF THE SOFT-
NESS AND BLURRED EDGES THEY GIVE TO THE
PATTERN OUTLINES.
I LIKE TO EXPLORE THE CONTRAST BETWEEN
'HARD' AND 'SOFT' IMAGES. FOR THE ROSE
JACKET, FOR EXAMPLE, I TOOK A TRADITIONAL
FULL-BLOWN ROSE AND COMBINED IT WITH A
BOLD GRAPHIC FLOURISH, LIKE SCRIBBLED
GRAFFITI. THE CONTRAST BETWEEN THE TWO
IS EXCITING, AND BOTH IMAGES ARE STRONG
ENOUGH TO BALANCE EACH OTHER.
MY AIM WITH FLORAL DESIGNS IS TO SIMPLIFY
YET STILL CAPTURE THE ESSENCE OF FLOWERS.
FOR EXAMPLE, THE IRIS DESIGN TRIES TO
CATCH EXACTLY THE FEELING OF A GROWING
FLOWER. THE COLOURING DOES NOT HAVE TO
BE NATURALISTIC – IN FACT IMAGINATIVE
HIGHLIGHTS MAKE THE WHOLE GARMENT MORE
ORIGINAL.
IN THE POSY TRELLIS, THE SAME 'HARD AND
SOFT' IDEA, IS EXPRESSED BY THE NATURAL-
ISTIC, UNEVEN LEAF FORMS AGAINST A STRUC-
TURED BACKGROUND GRID, REPEATED TO GIVE
AN INTENSELY PATTERNED EFFECT. THIS DE-
SIGN ALSO EMPHASIZES THE INTERPLAY OF
BACKGROUND AND FOREGROUND, WITH THE
FLOWERS OF THE POSIES EMBROIDERED IN
THREE-DIMENSIONAL REALITY ONTO THE BACK-
GROUND LEAVES
FOR THE TRAILING ROSES DESIGN, I WANTED
TO CREATE A FEELING OF LOOKING INTO A
TRELLIS OVERGROWN WITH ROSES, AN IMAGE
ENHANCED BY THE USE AGAIN OF ANGORA OR
MOHAIR. I HAVE FOUND THAT THE COLOURING
IN THIS DESIGN IS BEST KEPT PRETTY AND
NATURALISTIC, BUT DON'T BE AFRAID TO TRY
OUT YOUR OWN IDEAS.

ROSE JACKET

The Kimono style jacket is knitted in Mohair in stocking stitch from charts. It is worked in simple panels alternating the rose motif with the scribble motif, and is equally effective in a variety of different colourways.

SIZE
One size to fit up to 38in/97cm bust loosely.
Knitted measurements: all round width at underarm 56in/142cm; length 30in/76cm; sleeve length 13in/33cm.

ABBREVIATIONS
See page 15.

MATERIALS
○ 29 × 25g balls of Mohair in 5 colours as follows:

  15 balls main colour (MC), shown here black
  8 balls in first contrast (A) for edgings and motif, shown here grey
  2 balls each of 2 flower colours (B and C), here mulberry and pink
  2 balls in green (Gn) for leaves

○ 3 large buttons
○ One pair of needles is required in the size to give correct tension
○ Medium crochet hook
○ Suggested colourways:
  a)   MC = black,   A = grey,   B = pink, C = mulberry, Gn = sea green
  b)   MC = grey or pink,   A = black, B = turquoise, C = blue, Gn = fern green
  c)   MC = white,   A = grey,   B = lilac, C = turquoise, Gn = sea green

TENSION
Measured over st st, 16 sts and 20 rows to 4in/10cm using 5½mm (UK size 5) needles or the size to give correct tension.
To avoid disappointment, it is essential to check your tension carefully before commencing the garment and use the needles which give **you** the correct tension. **This may not be the size quoted in the standard tension**, as individual knitters vary.
How to check tension: using the recommended needles and a light colour, cast on 24 sts and work in st st for 30 rows. Cast off. Pin the square down flat without stretching. Place a pin between 2 sts near the left, count 16 sts and mark with another pin between the 16th and 17th sts. Mark out 20 rows in the same way. Measure the distance between pins. This should be 4in/10cm in both directions. If it is less your knitting is too tight – try one size larger needle. If it is more, your knitting is too loose – try one size smaller needle. Repeat the process until the correct tension is achieved. Do not be afraid to go up or down more than one needle size.

NOTES ON WORKING PATTERN
One square of chart represents one stitch. Odd numbered rows (rs) are knit – read from right to left; even numbered rows (ws) are purl – read from left to right. Use a separate ball of MC for each side of rose, and a small ball of Gn for each leaf. Use one ball of B and C for rose, and weave in colour not in use **loosely** at the back. Use separate long lengths of A for details at each side of rose. Use one ball of MC throughout the scribble motif, stranded loosely across, but use separate small balls of A for each main section of scribble. Cross yarns when changing colour to link colours and prevent holes appearing in the knitting. Take great care not to pull the colours at the back too tight as this will distort the knitting.

BACK
Knitted in 2 panels of 58 sts each.
Panel 1: With MC, cast on 58 sts and work 4 rows st st, starting with a knit row. Start working from chart at row 5 as follows, joining in and breaking off yarns as necessary.
Row 5: knit 27MC, 3A, 13MC, 1A, 14MC.
Row 6: purl 13MC, 3A, 11MC, 5A, 26MC.
Cont working from chart until row 90 is complete. Return to row 5 of chart and work to row 47. Work 8 more rows in MC in st st. Cast off.
Panel 2: with MC, cast on 58 sts and work 5 rows st st, starting with a k row. Start working from chart at row 48 as follows:
Row 48: purl 33MC, 1Gn, 24MC.
Cont from chart until row 90 is complete. Return to row 5 and work to row 90 again.

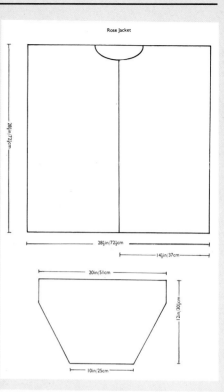

Rose Jacket

Work 7 rows in MC in st st.
Cast off.

LEFT FRONT

Work as Panel 2 of back until row 83 of second rose motif is complete.
Shape neck: cast off 9 sts at beg of next row. Cont in patt, but dec 1 st at neck edge of next 9 rows. 44 sts.
Work 4 rows straight in st st and cast off.

RIGHT FRONT

Work as Panel 1 of back until row 40 of second scribble motif is complete.
Shape neck: as left front.
Work 5 rows straight in st st and cast off.

LEFT SLEEVE (Scribble Motif)

With MC cast on 40 sts and knit 1 row. Inc 1 st at each end of next and every alt row until there are 52 sts, ending on a purl row. Start scribble motif as follows:
Next row: knit 23MC, 3A, 13MC, 1A, 12MC.
Next row: inc in first st, purl 10MC, 3A, 11MC, 5A, 21MC, inc in last st.
Cont scribble motif from chart (starting at row 7) but cont to inc at each side on every p row until there are 80 sts. Cont working scribble motif from chart with no further shaping until row 47 has been completed.
Work 5 rows more in st st. Cast off.
Lengthen sleeve, if preferred, by working straight in st st for required length.

RIGHT SLEEVE (Rose Motif)

With MC cast on 40 sts and knit 1 row. Inc 1 st at each end of next and every alt row until there are 50 sts, ending with a knit row. Start rose motif as follows:
Next row: inc in first st, purl 29MC, 1Gn, 18MC, inc in last st.
Next row: knit 20MC, 2Gn, 30MC.
Next row: inc in first st, purl 27MC, 4Gn, 19MC, inc in last st. 54 sts.
Cont rose motif from chart (starting at row 51), but cont to inc 1 st at each side on every purl row until there are 80 sts. Cont working rose motif from chart with no further shaping until row 90 is complete.
Work 6 rows more in st st, and cast off.

EDGINGS

With A, cast on 8 sts and work in st st for 111in/282cm, or until edging fits all round front and bottom edges when slightly stretched. Leave sts on a thread.
Cuff edging: work 2 strips of 8in/20cm as given above.
Collar: using A, cast on 22 sts and work in st st for 19in/48cm. Cast off.

FINISHING

Do not press. Darn in all loose ends carefully. Sew back panels together with panel 1 at the left. Using backstitch seams, join shoulder seams and sew sleeves to body, matching centre of sleeve to shoulder seam. With rs tog, back stitch cuff edging around cuff, turn in half to inside and slip st in place. Join side and sleeve seams. With rs tog, starting at neck, tack edging in place all round front and lower edges, easing round bottom corners and slightly stretching along bottom edge of back. Sew in place and slip st to inside. Sew on collar in same way. Neaten edges of collar and bindings. With crochet hook, work 3 button loops of 10 chain sts to lay flat along edge, positioned at top edge and between the motifs. Sew on buttons.

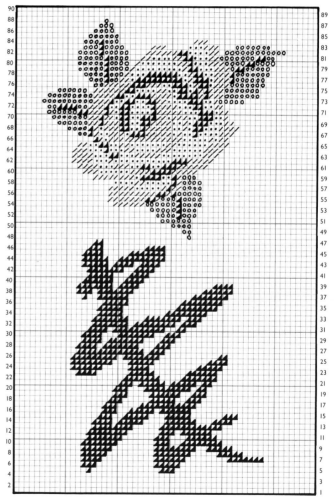

☐	= main colour [black]
◪	= A [grey]
▨	= B [pink]
⊡	= C [mulberry]
◎	= Gn [sea green]

IRIS

Two versions of this cardigan are shown, one in Mohair and one in 100% Angora, both knitted from exactly the same pattern, with only an adjustment in needle size. There are different iris sprays on back and front, knitted from the charts in stocking stitch, balanced by plain sleeves. The cardigan looks pretty knitted in black, white or grey, with either bright or subtle colours for the flowers themselves.

SIZES

There are 2 sizes to fit up to 35in/89cm or up to 38in/97cm bust.

Knitted measurements: width at underarm 19 [20½]in/48 [52]cm; length 22½ [23½]in/57 [60]cm; sleeve length 22½ [23]in/57 [58½]cm.

ABBREVIATIONS

See page 15.

MATERIALS

○ 21 [22] × 25g balls of Mohair or 21 [22] × 20g balls of 100% Angora in 5 colours as follows:

  15 [16] balls in main colour, black, grey or white (MC)
  2 balls each in green (Gn) and blue (Bl)
  1 ball each in pink (Pk) and red (Rd)

○ 9 buttons

○ 2 pairs of needles are required, one pair for st st parts in size to give correct tension; one pair 2 sizes smaller for ribbing (3 sizes smaller for Angora version)

TENSION

Measured over st st, 16 sts and 20 rows to 4in/10cm using 5½mm (UK size 5) needles for Mohair version, or 6mm (UK size 4) needles for Angora version. Recommended needles for ribbing (both versions): 4½mm (UK size 7). To avoid disappointment, it is essential to check your tension carefully before commencing the garment and use the needles which give **you** the correct tension. **This may not be the size quoted in the standard tension**, as individual knitters vary.

How to check tension: Using the recommended needles and a light colour, cast on 24 sts and work in st st for 30 rows. Cast off. Pin the square down flat without stretching. Place a pin between 2 sts near the left, count 16 sts and mark with another pin between the 16th and 17th sts. Mark out 20 rows in the same way. Measure the distance between pins. This should be 4in/10cm in both directions. If it is less your knitting is too tight – try one size larger needle. It is more, your knitting is too loose – try one size smaller needle. Repeat the process until the correct tension is achieved. Do not be afraid to go up or down more than one needle size. Adjust the size of the second pair of needles accordingly.

NOTES ON WORKING PATTERN

One square of chart represents one stitch. Odd numbered rows (rs) are knit – read from right to left; even numbered rows (ws) are purl – read from left to right. Use a separate ball or length of yarn for each area of colour, especially on either side of stems of Iris design, and avoid stranding yarn across back of work. Cross yarns where they meet when changing colour to link colours and prevent gaps appearing in the knitting. Take care not to pull the colours at the back too tight or this will distort the knitting. You will find it helpful to wind small bobbins (made from card) of the colours to prevent tangling. Allow them to hang close to the needle and unravel small amounts as needed.

Angora version only: work all ribs in twisted k1, p1 rib by working all knit sts into the **back** of the stitch.

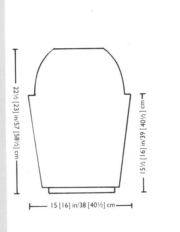
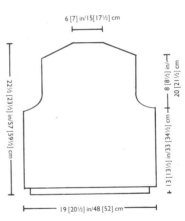
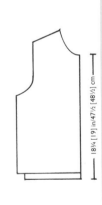

6 [7] in/15 [17½] cm

22½ [23] in/57 [58½] cm

15½ [16] in/39 [40½] cm

15 [16] in/38 [40½] cm

22½ [23½] in/57 [59½] cm

8 [8½] in/20 [21½] cm

13 [13½] in/33 [34½] cm

19 [20½] in/48 [52] cm

18¾ [19] in/47½ [48½] cm

BACK

Using the smaller needles and MC, cast on 69 [74] sts and work in k1, p1 rib for 1in/2½cm.

Increase row: purl, working twice into first and every foll 10th st. 76 [82] sts.

Change to the larger needles. Start working from chart for back at row 1 (bottom right) as follows:

Row 1: knit 30 [33]MC, 3Gn, 2MC, 4Gn, 4MC, 3Gn, 30 [33]MC.

Row 2: purl 30 [33]MC, 3Gn, 4MC, 4Gn, 2MC, 3Gn, 30 [33]MC.

Cont in patt from chart until row 60 [62] is complete.

Shape armholes: cast off 3 sts at beg of next 2 rows and 2 sts at beg of foll 2 rows. Dec 1 st at beg of foll 6 rows. 60 [66] sts. Cont straight in patt until row 100 [104] is complete. (Back measures 21 [22]in/53½ [56]cm from beg.)

Shape shoulders: cast off 5 sts at beg of next 6 rows and 4 [6] sts at beg of next 2 rows. Leave rem 22 [24] sts on holder for neckband.

FRONTS

Using the smaller needles and MC, cast on 36 [38] sts and work in k1, p1 rib for 1in/2½cm.

Increase row: purl, working twice into every 10th st, 38 [41] sts. Change to the larger needles and start working from appropriate chart at row 1. Cont until row 60 [62] (left) or row 61 [63] (right) is complete.

Shape armhole: cast off 3 sts at beg of next row and 2 sts at beg of foll alt row. Dec 1 st at side edge of foll 3 alt rows. 30 [33] sts.

Cont until row 89 [91] (left) or row 90 [92] (right) is complete.

Shape neck: cast off 5 [7] sts at beg of next row. Dec 1 st at neck edge of foll 6 [5] rows. 19 [21] sts. Work 4 [7] more rows.

Shape shoulder: cast off 5 sts at beg of next and foll 2 alt rows. Work 1 row. Cast off rem sts.

SLEEVES

Using the smaller needles and MC, cast on
36 [38] sts and work in k1, p1 rib for 1in/2½cm.
Increase row: purl, working twice into
every 3rd st. 48 [50] sts. Change to the larger
needles and work in st st, inc 1 st at each end
of next and every foll 12th [11th] row until
there are 60 [64] sts. Work straight until
sleeve measures 15½ [16]in/39½ [40½]cm from
beg.
Shape top: cast off 3 sts at beg of next 2 rows.
Dec 1 st at each end of every 5th row until
there are 44[48] sts. Work 2 rows. Dec 1 st at
each end of next and every foll row until
30 [32] sts remain. Cast off.

NECKBAND

Join shoulder seams using backstitch. With rs
facing, using the smaller needles and MC, knit
up approx 64 [68] sts around neck edge
(22 [24] from back, 21 [22] from each front).
Work in k1, p1 rib for 1in/2½cm. Cast off in
rib.

FRONT BANDS

Left: With rs facing, using the smaller needles
and MC, knit up 88 [90] sts along front edge,
including neckband. Work in k1, p1 rib for
1in/2½cm. Cast off loosely in rib.
Right: Work as left but make 9 buttonholes
in centre of band as follows:
Rib 3 rows.
1st buttonhole row: rib 3 [4], (cast off 2 sts,
rib 8 including st used in casting off) 8 times,
cast off 2 sts, rib 3 [4].
2nd buttonhole row: rib, casting on 2 sts
over those sts cast off in previous row.

FINISHING

Do not press. Darn in all loose ends carefully,
closing up any gaps. Using backstitch seams,
join side and sleeve seams. Set in sleeves
making 4 small pleats in the sleeve head to fit
into armhole. Sew on buttons.

BACK

⊠	= blue or A
⊘	= green or B
⊡	= pink or C
◪	= red or D
☐	= main colour MC

RIGHT FRONT

LEFT FRONT

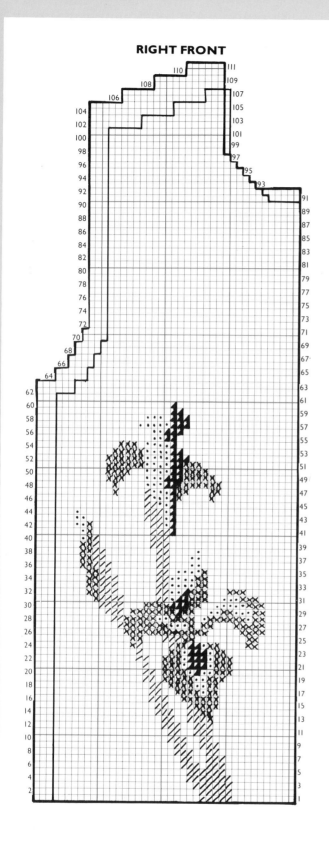

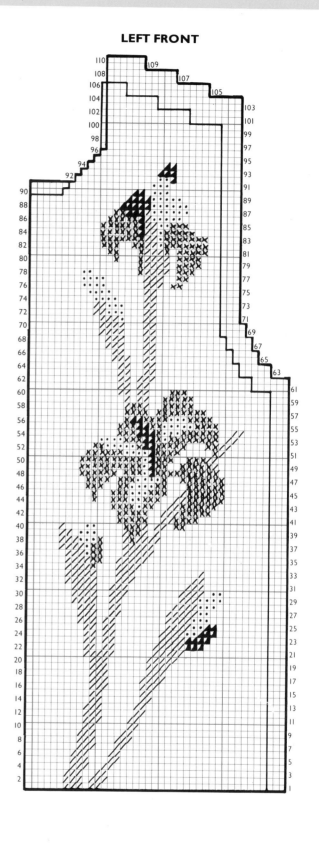

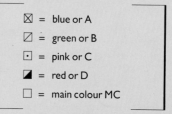

⊠	=	blue or A
⧄	=	green or B
·	=	pink or C
◥	=	red or D
☐	=	main colour MC

IRIS BATWING

This elegant batwing sweater is knitted in 100% Angora, in stocking stitch in one main piece. There are two iris sprays knitted from a chart on the front, and a plain back. The main piece is knitted from cuff to cuff, with waist ribbing added later so the design is actually knitted sideways. For a plain version of this design, simply omit the flowers from the front.

SIZES
One size to fit up to 38in/97cm bust.
Knitted measurements: width from cuff to cuff 59in/150cm; length 26in/66cm.

ABBREVIATIONS
See page 15.

MATERIALS
○ 24 × 20g balls of 100% Angora yarn in colours as follows:
    20 balls in main colour, MC
    1 ball each in 4 contrast colours A, B, C, D
○ 2 pairs of needles are required, one pair for main parts in the size to give the correct tension; one pair 2 sizes smaller for ribbing
○ 2 stitch holders
○ medium crochet hook

TENSION
Measured over st st, 18 sts and 22 rows to 4in/10cm using 5½mm (UK size 5) needles or the size to give correct tension. Recommended needles for edgings: 4½mm (UK size 7).
To avoid disappointment, it is essential to check your tension carefully before commencing the garment and use the needles which give **you** the correct tension. **This may not be the size quoted in the standard tension**, as individual knitters vary.
How to check tension: Using the recommended needles and Angora, cast on 28 sts and work in st st for 6in/15cm. Cast off. Pin the square down flat without stretching. Place a pin between 2 sts near the left, count 18 sts and mark with another pin between the 18th and 19th sts. Mark out 22 rows in the same way. Measure the distance between pins. This should be 4in/10cm in both directions. If it is less your knitting is too tight – try one size larger needle. If it is more, your knitting is too loose – try one size smaller needle. Repeat the process until the correct tension is achieved. Do not be afraid to go up or down more than one needle size. Adjust the size of the second pair of needles accordingly.

NOTES ON WORKING PATTERN
One square of chart represents one stitch. Odd numbered rows(rs) are knit – read from right to left; even numbered rows (ws) are

purl – read from left to right. Use a separate ball or length of yarn for each area of colour, and cross the yarns when changing colour to link the colours and prevent holes appearing in the knitting. To minimize tangling of colours, wind small bobbins (which can be made from card) of each colour, and allow these to hang close to the needle, just unravelling a small amount at a time as required.

MAIN PIECE
Using the larger needles and MC, cast on 30 sts. Working in st st throughout proceed as follows:
Starting with a knit row, inc 1st at each end of every 4th row until there are 50 sts. Work 3 rows straight, then inc 1 st at each end of every row until there are 188 sts. Cast on 10 sts at beg of next 2 rows, rs of work is facing for next row. 208 sts. Now introduce pattern on right half of piece (front), working these

sts from chart, beg at row 1 as follows (note chart sts are bracketed):

Row 1: knit (104 sts MC), 104 sts MC.
Row 2: purl 104MC, (54MC, 1B, 49MC).
Row 3: knit (48MC, 1B, 55MC), 104MC.
Row 4: purl 104MC, (56MC, 1B, 47MC).
Row 5: knit (46MC, 1B, 16MC, 2A, 39MC), 104MC.

Cont in this way until row 24 of chart has been worked, rs facing.

Divide for neck: Work 104 sts from row 25 of chart and turn, leaving rem sts on a spare needle. Cont working from chart on these sts only until row 75 is completed. Break yarn and return to sts on spare needle for back. Work 51 rows st st on this second set of sts only, so ending with a k row.

Next row: p104, patt 104 sts from row 76 of chart. 208 sts.

Cont in patt over all sts as before, working from row 77 to row 100 to chart.

Cast off 10 sts at beg of next 2 rows. 188 sts. Dec 1 st at each end of every row until there are 50 sts. Work 3 rows straight. Now dec 1 st at each end of next and every foll 4th row until 30 sts remain. Work 3 rows straight. Cast off.

Note: for a plain sweater, omit the colours in instructions above and work entirely in MC.

WAISTBAND

Back and front are knitted separately. Using the smaller needles and MC, with rs facing, knit up 66 sts evenly from straight edge of back or front. Work in k1, p1 rib for 3in/7½cm. Cast off loosely in rib.

FINISHING

Do not press. Using backstitch seams, join side seams excluding ribbing. Neatly oversew waistband seams. Work a row of double crochet around each cuff to neaten, but just allow the neck edges to roll naturally inwards.

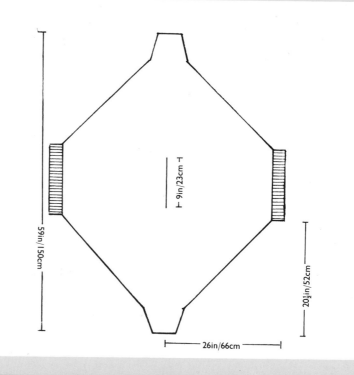

FRONT

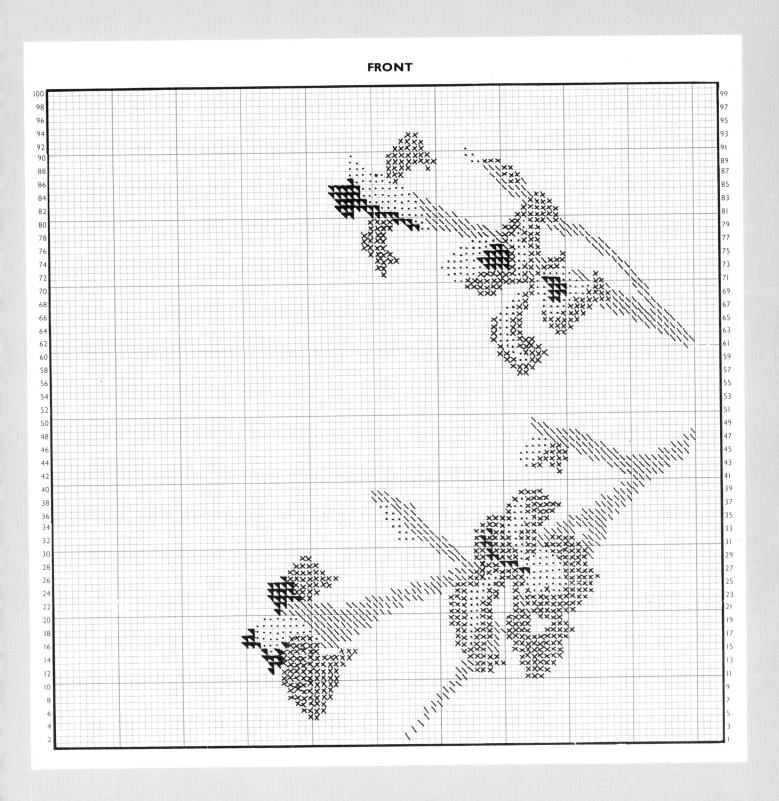

⊠ = blue or A

⬈ = green or B

⊡ = pink or C

◣ = red or D

☐ = main colour MC

POSY TRELLIS

For this loose fitting cardigan I have used a textured cotton to give extra surface interest. The repeated posy motif of knitted leaves and embroidered flowers on the diamond trellis creates a continuous pattern over the whole garment. It is knitted from the chart mainly in fairisle in Rowan Salad Days Cotton. I outlined the cabled edgings in black to give the shape extra definition, and made the fronts wider than the back to give the cardigan an attractively draped line from the padded shoulders.

SIZE
One size to fit up to 38in/97cm bust. The shoulder width is adjusted to fit during making up.
Knitted measurements: all round width at underarm 44in/112cm; length 21in/53cm; sleeve length 23½in/59½cm.

ABBREVIATIONS
See page 15.

MATERIALS
○ 15 × 50g balls of Rowan's Salad Days Cotton in 7 colours as follows:
  12 balls of main colour (A), grey, white or black
  5 balls of first contrast colour (B), black or grey
  4 balls of second contrast (J), jade for leaves
  1 ball each or oddments of 4 further colours, bright pink, sunshine, hyacinth and cream for flowers
○ 9 buttons
○ 2 pairs of needles are required, one pair for fairisle parts in the size to give correct tension; one pair 2 sizes smaller for edgings
○ one cable needle
○ large-eyed yarn needle
○ medium crochet hook
○ one pair shoulder pads (optional)

TENSION
Measured over fairisle diamond pattern, 26 sts and 26 rows to 4in/10cm using 4mm (UK size 8) needles or the size to give correct tension. Recommended needles for edgings 3¼mm (UK size 10).
To avoid disappointment it is essential to check your tension carefully before starting the garment, and use the needles which give **you** the correct tension. **This may not be** the size quoted in the standard tension as individual knitters vary.
How to check tension: using the recommended needles and A, cast on 40 sts and purl 1 row. Join in B and work as follows in st st, starting with a k row:
Row 1(rs): knit (1B, 7A) 5 times.
Row 2(ws): purl (1B, 5A, 1B, 1A) 5 times.
Row 3: knit (2A, 1B, 1A) 10 times.
Row 4: purl (2A, 1B, 1A, 1B, 3A) 5 times.

Row 5: knit (4A, 1B, 3A) 5 times.
Row 6: as row 4.
Row 7: as row 3.
Row 8: as row 2.
Repeat rows 1 to 8 four times more and cast off. Pin the piece down flat without stretching. Place a pin between 2 sts near the left, count 26 sts, and mark with another pin between the 26th and 27th sts. Mark out 26 rows in the same way. Measure the distance between pins. This should be 4in/10cm in both directions. If it is less your knitting is too tight – try one size larger needle. If it is more, your knitting is too loose — try one size smaller needle. Repeat the process until the correct tension is achieved. Do not be afraid to go up or down more than one needle size. Adjust the size of the second pair of needles accordingly.

NOTES ON WORKING PATTERN
One square of chart represents one stitch. Odd numbered rows (rs) are knit – read from right to left; even numbered rows (ws) are purl – read from left to right. When working diamond pattern, strand colour B **loosely** at the back of the work, or weave in once behind centre st of diamond. Use a separate length of J (of approx 112in/285cm) for each group of leaves, and weave in A and B at the back.

BACK
Using the smaller needles and B, cast on 141 sts and work as follows:
Row 1(rs): p1, (k4, p1) to end.
Row 2(ws): k1, (p4, k1) to end.
Row 3: change to A, work as row 1.
Row 4: as row 2.

Row 5: p1, (c4b, p1) to end.
Cont in A, work rows 2 to 5, then rows 2 and 3.**
Change to the larger needles and purl 1 row. inc 5 sts evenly across the row, 146 sts. Join in B and work in fairisle patt from chart starting at row 1 as follows:
Row 1: knit 6AL, (1B, 7A) rep to last 4 sts, 1B, 3A.
Row 2: purl 2A, (1B, 1A, 1B, 5A) rep to end.
Cont in patt from chart to row 8 then join in 3 separate lengths of J for each motif on row 9. Cont straight in patt until row 76 is complete. (Work measures 13in/33cm from beg.)
Shape armholes: cast off 6 sts at beg of next 2 rows, then 4 sts, then 3 sts, then 2 sts. Dec 1 st at each end of foll alt row, 4 times, 108 sts. Cont straight until row 125 is complete.
Divide for neck and shoulders: patt 35 sts and turn. Work 3 rows more and cast off. Rejoin yarn to neck edge, ws facing, cast off centre 38 sts, patt to end. Work 3 rows and cast off.

LEFT FRONT
Using the smaller needles and B, cast on 71 sts and work cable rib as given for back to **.
Change to the larger needles and purl 1 row, inc 1 st at each end of row. 73 sts. Work in patt from chart until row 76 is complete.
Shape armhole: cast off 6 sts at beg of next row, and dec 1 st at beg of foll 4 alt rows. 63 sts. Work straight until row 105 is complete.
Shape neck: cast off 10 sts at beg of next row. Dec 1 st at neck edge of every foll row, 9 times. 44 sts. Cont straight until row 129 is complete. Cast off leaving a thread of approx 15in/38cm.

LEFT FRONT

RIGHT FRONT

BACK AND FRONTS

□ = A [main colour]
◉ = B [1st contrast]
· = J [jade]
——— = back
—— = front

RIGHT FRONT

Work as left front, but reverse shaping as follows:
Shape armholes after 77th row, and neck after 106th row.

SLEEVES

Using the smaller needles and B, cast on 56 sts and work cable rib as given for back to **. Change to the larger needles and purl 1 row, inc 1 st at each end. 58 sts. Start patt from row 1 of chart with a knit row, inc 1 st at each end of 3rd and every foll alt row to 86 sts. Inc 1 st each end of every foll 4th row to 108 sts. Work straight until row 92 is complete. (Work measures 15½in/39cm from beg.)
Shape top: cast off 4 sts at beg of next 2 rows. Dec 1 st at each end of next and every foll alt row to 58 sts, then dec 1 st at each end of every row to row 143. 42 sts. Cast off.

FRONT BANDS

Work these separately, or knit up sts from front edge as preferred. Using the smaller needles and A, either knit up (rs facing), or cast on 131 sts.
Row 1(ws): k1, (p4, k1) to end.
Row 2(rs): p1, (k4, p1) to end.
Row 3: as row 1.
Row 4: p1, (c4b, p1) to end.
Row 5 to 7: rep rows 1 to 3.
Row 8: change to B, work as row 4.
Row 9: as row 1.
Cast off knitwise, **decreasing** as follows: knit the 5th and 6th and every foll 4th and 5th sts together before casting off.

NECKBAND

Using the smaller needles and A, either knit up around neck edge including both front bands, or cast on 131 sts and work as given for front bands.

FINISHING

Lightly press the pieces using a steam iron or damp cloth and darn in loose ends.
Embroidery: using the large-eyed needle, and the four colours pink, sunshine, hyacinth and cream, work 10 or 11 French knots in clusters of 2 or 3 of each colour in the centre of each group of leaves. Use a single strand of yarn and approx 6 twists around the needle. Vary the arrangement within the posies throughout (see photograph for guidance).
To finish: slightly gather up the top edge of each front, to match the back shoulders, using the thread left for this purpose. Using backstitch seams, join shoulder seams. Join side seams, taking care to match pattern. Join

sleeve seams. Set in sleeves, making 2 pleats at either side of, and facing away from, the shoulder seam. If necessary, oversew front bands and neckband in place. Using crochet hook and B, work a row of double crochet along ends of cable bands to complete contrast edging. Place 9 pins evenly spaced along left front band and sew on buttons. Work crochet chain loops in B along right front edge to correspond with buttons and fasten off securely (see diagram).
Shoulders: if necessary, reduce the width across the shoulders as follows: take in each side by making one or two pleats over the shoulder seam, pin in position and topstitch each pleat for 1½in/4cm on front and back using matching sewing thread.
Optional shoulder pads: Insert triangular shoulder pads to emphasize shoulder line.

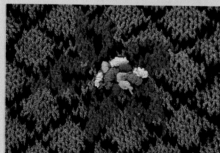

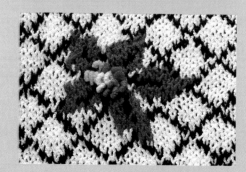

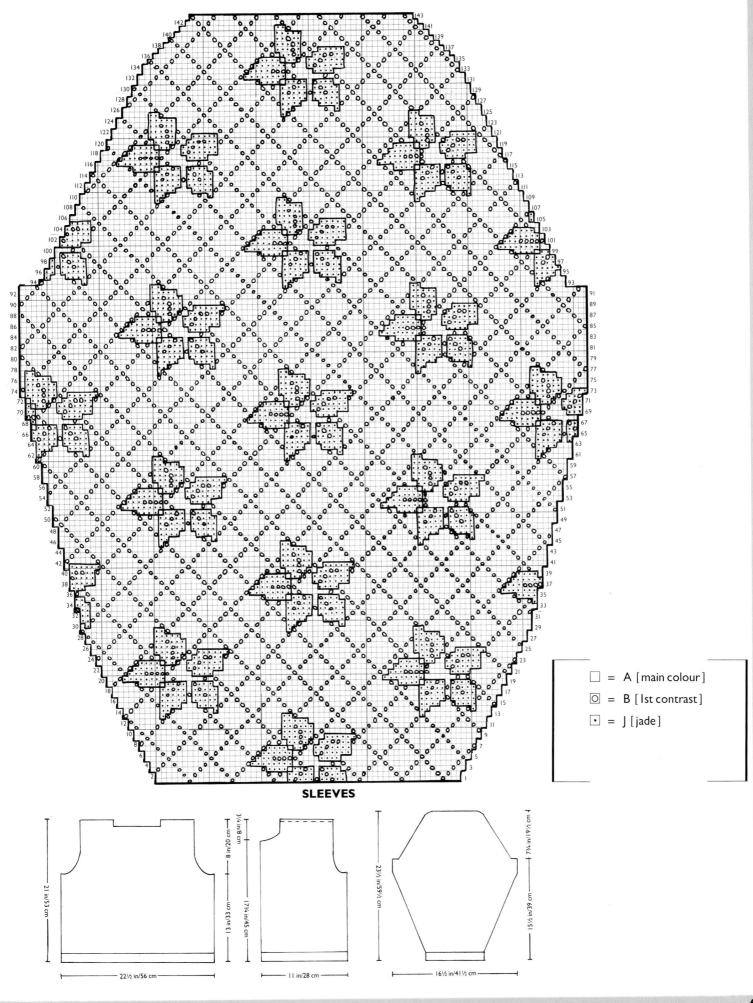

SLEEVES

□ = A [main colour]

⊙ = B [1st contrast]

⦁ = J [jade]

TRAILING ROSES SWEATER

These two variations show how two diverse moods can be created from the same design. The evening jacket, knitted in 100% Angora, is pure luxury, whilst the sweater knitted in Mohair is much more casual for everyday wear, sized to be large and comfortable. Both styles are knitted in stocking stitch in fairisle, the jacket is trimmed with garter stitch, and the sweater with ribbing. As with other Angora designs, the jacket can also be made in the Mohair yarn.

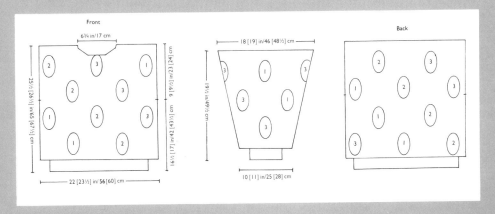

SIZES
There are two generous sizes to fit up to 36in/91cm or up to 38in/97cm bust.
Knitted measurements: width at underarm 22 [23½]in/56 [60]cm; length 25½ [26½]in/65 [67½]cm, sleeve length 19½in/49½cm.

ABBREVIATIONS
See page 15.

MATERIALS
○ 26 [28] × 25g balls of Mohair in 5 colours as follows:
  14 [15] balls of main colour (MC), black, grey or white
  9 [10] balls of green (G)
  1 ball each of 3 flower colours, (A), (B) and (C)
○ 2 pairs of needles are required, one pair for main parts in the size to give the correct tension; one pair 2 sizes smaller for edgings
○ 1 circular needle or set of 4 double-pointed needles in smaller size
○ stitch holder

TENSION
Measured over fairisle pattern, 18 sts and 18 rows to 4in/10cm, using 6mm (UK size 4 needles) or the size to give the correct tension. Recommended needles for edging: 5mm (UK size 6).
To avoid disappointment, it is essential to check your tension carefully before commencing the garment and use the needles which give **you** the correct tension. **This may not be the size quoted in the standard tension**, as individual knitters vary.
How to check tension: Read Notes on working pattern. Using the recommended needles and MC, cast on 30 sts and work tension square from the chart for . back, starting with a knit row at row 1, working from sts 1 to 30. Work in st st until row 30 is complete, then cast off loosely. Pin the square down flat without stretching. Place a pin between 2 sts near the left, count 18 sts and place another pin between the 18th and 19th sts. Mark out 18 rows in the same way. Measure the distance between the pins. This should be 4in/10cm in both directions. If

it is less your knitting is too tight – try one size larger needle. If it is more, your knitting is too loose – try one size smaller needle. Repeat the process until the correct tension is achieved. Do not be afraid to go up or down more than one needle size. Adjust the size of the second pair of needles accordingly.

NOTES ON WORKING PATTERN
One square of chart represents one stitch. Odd numbered rows (rs) are knit – read from right to left; even numbered rows (ws) are purl – read from left to right. Use one ball of MC and one ball of G across the width of the knitting and weave in **loosely** at the back of every 4th st. Use separate lengths of yarn for flower colours and weave MC and G behind the flowers, taking care not to pull too tightly.
Note: all flowers are **not** the same. Flowers are worked in 3 colour combinations using two of the three colours A, B or C in each flower. Flowers are as follows, worked in diagonal lines as per diagram:

Flower colourway	1	2	3
Outer × =	red (or A)	pink (or B)	mulberry (or C)
Inner ◢ =	pink (or B)	mulberry (or C)	red (or A)

BACK
Using the smaller needles and MC, cast on 68 [80] sts and work in k2, p2 twisted rib (i.e. k2, p2 rib with every k st worked into the back of the st) for 2½ [3]in/6½ [7½]cm, ending with a rs row.
Increase row: Change to the larger needles and purl, working twice into 4th [1st] st and every foll alt [3rd] st to last 4 [1] sts, purl to end. 99 [107] sts.*
Begin working from chart for back at row 1 with a knit row, joining in colours as indicated on the diagram. Cont straight from chart, placing markers for armholes at 16½ [17]in/42 [43]cm from beg. Cont in patt without shaping until row 105 [109] of chart is complete. Cast off loosely placing markers on 34th [38th] st and 66th [70th] st for neck opening.

FRONT
Work as for back to *. Begin working from

chart at row 1 with a knit row and cont straight until row 96 [98] is complete.
Shape neck: Row 97 [99]: patt 41 [45], turn and leave rem 58 [62] sts on a st holder. Cont working on these 41 [45] sts for first side of neck, dec 1 st at neck edge of next 7 rows. Work straight until row 105 [109] is complete. Cast off loosely.
Replace sts from st holder onto needle. With rs facing, rejoin yarn and cast off next 17 sts and patt to end. Cont working on these sts, for second side of neck, dec 1 st at neck edge of next 7 rows. Work straight until row 105 [109] is complete. Cast off loosely.

SLEEVES
Using the smaller needles and MC, cast on 32 [36] sts and work in k2, p2 twisted rib as before for 2in/5cm, ending with a rs row. Change to the larger needles.
Increase row: purl, working twice into 5th and every foll alt st to last 3 sts, p3. 45 [51] sts. Beg working from chart for sleeve at row 1 with a knit row, following appropriate outline.
Shape sleeves: cont in patt, inc 1 st at each end of 6th and every foll 4th row to 81 [88] sts, incorporating extra sts into patt. Cont straight until row 80 is complete or work measures 19½in/49½cm. Cast off loosely.

COLLAR
Using backstitch, join shoulder seams.
Using MC and the circular needle, rs facing, knit up 80 [84] sts around neck edge, starting and finishing at the centre front as follows: 23 [24] sts from right front, 34 [36] sts from back neck, 23 [24] sts from left front. Work 4 rounds in k2, p2 twisted rib, then work in rows back and forth, dividing at centre front, until collar measures 4in/10cm. Cast off loosely in rib.
Alternative method: work the collar separately on 2 needles and oversew onto neck edge with opening at centre front. Join the first 4 rows of collar at centre front.

FINISHING
Darn in all loose ends. Do not press. Using backstitch join sleeves to body between markers. Join side and sleeve seams.

1st size sweater back 99 sts

2nd size sweater back 107 sts

right front jacket 52 sts

left front jacket 52 sts

1st size sweater sleeve

2nd size sweater sleeve

☐ = MC

⊡ = G

⊠ = outer colour A, B or C

◪ = inner colour, B, C or A

TRAILING ROSES JACKET

For Tension and Notes on Working Pattern see Sweater instructions.

SIZES
One size to fit up to 38in/97cm bust. The shoulders are adjusted to fit during making up.
Knitted measurements: back width at underarm 23in/58cm; length 23½in/60cm; sleeve length 24in/61cm.

ABBREVIATIONS
See page 15.

MATERIALS
○ Either 30×20g balls of 100% Angora or 30×25g balls of Mohair in colours as follows:
   19 balls in main colour (MC)
   8 balls of green (G)
   1 ball in each of 3 flower colours, A, B, C
○ 2 buttons
○ 2 pairs of needles are required, one pair for st st parts in the size to give the correct tension; one pair 2 sizes smaller for edgings
○ one pair of shoulder pads

TENSION
Measured over fairisle pattern, 18 sts and 18 rows to 4in/10cm using 6mm (UK size 4) needles or the size to give correct tension. Recommended needles for edging: 5mm (UK size 6).

BACK
Using the smaller needles and MC, cast on 107 sts and work in g st for 1½in/4cm. Change to the larger needles and start patt at row 1 of chart with a knit row, joining in colours as required. Cont working from chart until row 64 is complete.
Shape armholes: Cast off 6 sts at beg of next 2 rows. Cast off 3 sts at beg of foll 4 rows. Dec 1 st at beg of next 6 rows (77 sts). Cont in patt

without shaping until row 95 of chart is complete.
Shape neck: Patt 27 sts, turn and work 4 rows more from chart on these sts, then cast off. With ws facing, rejoin yarn to neck, cast off centre 23 sts and patt to end. Work 4 rows more, cast off.

FRONTS
Using the smaller needles and MC, cast on 52 sts and work in g st for 1½in/4cm. Change to the larger needles and start working patt from chart for either right or left front at row 1 with a knit row, joining in colours as required. Cont working from chart until row 64 (left) or row 65 (right) is complete.
Shape armhole: Cast off 5 sts at beg of next row and 3 sts at beg of foll 2 alt rows. Dec 1 st at armhole edge of foll 3 alt rows (38 sts). Cont in patt without shaping until row 100 of

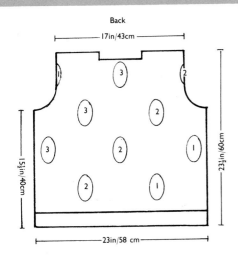

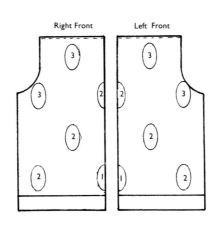

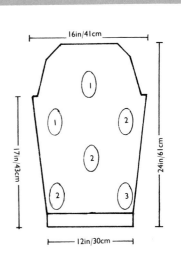

jacket sleeve 54 sts

1st size sweater front 99 sts

2nd size sweater front 107 sts
and
jacket back

☐ = MC

⊡ = G

⊠ = outer colour A, B or C

◧ = inner colour, B, C or A

chart is complete. Cast off loosely, leaving a long end of yarn, approx 15in/38cm.

SLEEVES

Using the smaller needles and MC, cast on 54 sts and work in g st for 1½in/4cm. Change to the larger needles and start working patt at row 1 of chart with a knit row, joining in colours as required. Shape sleeve by inc 1 st at each end of 6th and every foll 6th row until there are 74 sts. Cont in patt without shaping until row 70 of chart is complete.

- **Shape top:** cast off 3 sts at beg of next 2 rows, work 5 rows straight. Dec 1 st at each end of next row and every foll 5th row, three times. Dec 1 st at each end of every row until 40 sts rem and chart is complete. Cast off loosely.

FRONT EDGING AND COLLAR

Using the larger needles and MC, cast on 30 sts and work in g st until band fits around front and neck edges when **slightly** stretched (approx 50in/127cm). Leave sts on a length of yarn.

FINISHING

Run a gathering thread along the top edge of each front and draw up to match back shoulder width. Secure, and join shoulder seams using back stitch. Join side and sleeve seams, using back stitch — except for cuffs — oversew these. Adjust the width across back to fit by making 1 or 2 pleats across each shoulder from back to front, and topstitch in position using sewing thread. Set in sleeves, making surplus into 2 pleats at sleeve head, facing away from shoulder seam.

Pin edging all round front and neck edges and adjust the length by knitting extra or unravelling to ensure it is not too long or too short. Cast off. Oversew in place from the ws. Fold edging to rs and secure with a button at each front corner.

Shoulder pads: insert triangular shoulder pads to emphasize the square shoulder line, so they extend slightly beyond armhole seam. If knitted in Angora, this jacket is enhanced by inserting a lining made from fabric (silk if you can!). See page 14 for more details.

section 3

HERALDIC

THE RICH COLOURS AND FABULOUS IMAGERY OF HERALDRY HAVE INSPIRED MANY NEW DESIGNS – THE HERALDIC BEASTS SUCH AS LION, UNICORN AND GRIFFIN, THE SHIELDS AND SCROLLS, CROWNS AND ERMINE CAN BE USED TOGETHER FOR HIGHLY DECORATIVE EFFECTS. THE EVENING COAT SHOWN HERE, THE COAT OF ARMS, WAS PAINSTAKINGLY KNITTED BY THE INTARSIA METHOD OF MACHINE KNITTING, THEN EMBROIDERED TO COMPLETE THE DETAILS. IT HAS A SUMPTUOUS PURPLE LINING AND 'ERMINE' EDGING IN LUXURIOUS ANGORA – A REAL SHOW STOPPER!

FOR THE HANDKNITS IN THE FOLLOWING PAGES, I HAVE TAKEN THE DIFFERENT ELEMENTS, AND USED THEM IN VARYING SCALES. BECAUSE THE IMAGERY IS SO STRONG, I ADOPTED A GRAPHIC APPROACH TO THE DESIGNING, SO ALL THE PATTERNS ARE WORKED FROM CHARTS, AND I HAVE OFFSET THIS WITH CHANGES IN TEXTURE AND BOLD EDGINGS OF CABLES OR DIAGONAL RIB.

TO CARRY OFF SUCH STRONG DESIGNS, THE GARMENTS HAD TO BE LARGE AND RELAXED – NO ONE WILL HAVE PROBLEMS FINDING SOMETHING TO FIT! HOWEVER, THE SMALLER SIZE IS ACHIEVED ONLY BY CHANGE OF NEEDLE SIZE, SO WORKING TO TENSION IS AS IMPORTANT AS EVER FOR GOOD RESULTS. THE VIRTUE OF THIS METHOD IS THAT THE WHOLE GARMENT IS DECREASED TO SCALE, KEEPING THE PROPORTIONS CORRECTLY BALANCED.

I HAVE USED A DIFFERENT TREATMENT OF THE SHIELD SHAPE IN THE SMALL SHIELDS SWEATER – AS A REPEATED PATTERN MOTIF THE DESIGN ALSO EVOKES THE FEELING OF FLAGS AND SEMAPHORE IN THE DIVISION OF THE SHAPES AND PLACING OF COLOURS. THE VERY SIMPLE SWEATER SHAPE FITS EXACTLY THE LOGIC OF THE PATTERN, WHICH LOOKS EQUALLY GOOD IN MANY COLOURWAYS.

THE FLEUR DE LYS DESIGN IS BASED ON THE SAME SIMPLE SWEATER SHAPE AS SMALL SHIELDS, BUT HERE THE MOTIFS AND BACKGROUND ARE MORE EVENLY BALANCED. THE DESIGN IS SHOWN IN PALE COLOURS, BUT IF YOU USE THE BOLD PRIMARY COLOURS, IT WILL BECOME MORE 'HARLEQUIN' IN FEELING. MY OWN FAVOURITE DESIGN OF THE GROUP IS THE LION AND UNICORN SWEATER AND CARDIGAN – I GREATLY ENJOYED GETTING THE BEASTS JUST RIGHT, AND MADE THIS THE MOST COMPLEX OF THE GROUP BY INCLUDING ALL

THE HERALDIC ELEMENTS AT ONCE! THE PATTERN IS FAIRLY TIME-CONSUMING, BUT YOU COULD SIMPLIFY THE SWEATER (IF ABSOLUTELY NECESSARY) BY JUST KNITTING A PATTERNED FRONT. SOME CARE MUST BE TAKEN FOR A GOOD FINISH, BUT THE RESULT WILL BE A CLASSIC MASTERPIECE.

THE WHOLE GROUP OF DESIGNS IS KNITTED IN THE ROWAN SANDY BLACK WOOL TWIST RANGE, WITHIN WHICH THERE ARE TWO DISTINCT COLOUR CATEGORIES – THE INTENSE RICH COLOURS USED FOR MOST OF THE HERALDICS, AND THE SOFTER PALES WHICH I HAVE CHOSEN TO GIVE A COMPLETELY DIFFERENT LOOK. AS YOU CAN SEE, THE SHIELD DESIGN IS EXTREMELY SUCCESSFUL USING EITHER PALETTE – SO DO NOT BE TOO CONSTRAINED IN CHOOSING COLOURS.

LION AND UNICORN SWEATER AND CARDIGAN

This generously sized sweater and cardigan are knitted in Rowan Sandy Black Wool Twist in stocking stitch from charts. The design features motifs of heraldic creatures around a central shield, in all the rich colours of heraldry. Both versions are worked from the same basic chart. The sweater is identical on front and back, with bobble patterned sleeves reminiscent of ermine. The back of the man's cardigan uses the same design, which is complemented by crowns on the front borders and sleeves. Both styles are edged in cabled rib in the main colour. Colour variations are achieved by changing the main colour and sleeve colours, whilst keeping the central design the same.

SIZES
One large size to loosely fit up to 40in/102cm bust or up to 42in/107cm chest.
Knitted measurements: width at underarm 26½in/67cm; length 25in/63½cm (sweater), 27in/68½cm (cardigan); sleeve length 18in/46cm (sweater), 19in/48½cm (cardigan).

ABBREVIATIONS
See page 15.

MATERIALS
SWEATER
○24 × 50g balls of Rowan's Sandy Black Wool Twist in 7 colours as follows:
    8 balls main colour (MC) gold, purple, slate or claret (for edgings, sleeves and collar)
    3 balls each of Gold (Gd), Red (Rd), Emerald (Em)
    2 balls each of Claret (Ct), Blue (Bl), Purple (Pp)
    1 ball Mid Grey (MG)

CARDIGAN
○26 × 50g balls of Rowan's Sandy Black Wool Twist in 7 colours as follows:
    11 balls main colour (MC) as for sweater
    3 balls each of Gold (Gd), Emerald (Em), Red (Rd)
    2 balls each of Claret (Ct), Purple (Pp)
    1 ball each of Mid Grey (MG), Blue (Bl)
○7 buttons

BOTH STYLES
○2 pairs of needles are required, one pair for main parts in the size to give the correct tension; one pair 2 sizes smaller for edgings
○cable needle

TENSION
19 sts and 25 rows to 4in/10cm measured over st st patt using 5mm (UK size 6) needles. Recommended needles for edging – 4mm (UK size 8).
To avoid disappointment, it is essential to check your tension carefully before commencing the garment and to use the needles which give **you** the correct tension. **This may not be the size quoted in the standard tension**, as individual knitters vary.

How to check tension: Using 5mm (UK size 6) needles and MC, cast on 30 sts and joining in colours as required, work a section from chart as follows (see Notes on working pattern):
Starting from row 1 with a knit row, work from sts 1 to 30 on knit rows and 30 to 1 on purl rows, until row 35 is complete. Cast off loosely. **Lightly** steam press using steam iron or damp cloth. Pin square down flat without stretching. Place a pin between 2 sts near the left, count 19 sts and place another pin between the 19th and 20th sts. Mark out 25 rows in the same way. Measure the distance between pins. This should be 4in/10cm in both directions. If it is less, your knitting is too tight – try one size larger needle. If it is

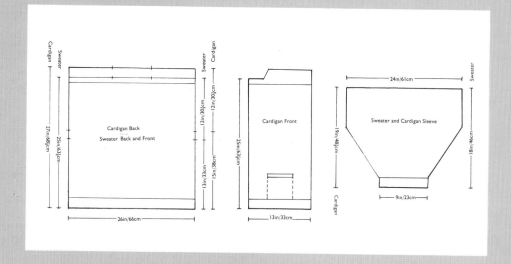

more, your knitting is too loose – try one size smaller. Repeat the process until the correct tension is achieved. Do not be afraid to go up or down more than one needle size. Adjust the size of the second pair of needles accordingly.

NOTES ON WORKING PATTERN
One square of chart represents one stitch. Odd numbered rows (rs) are knit – read from right to left; even numbered rows (ws) are purl – read from left to right. Use a separate ball or length of yarn for each main area of colour, **including** background colour each side of motif, and avoid stranding yarn across back of work. Cross yarns when changing colour to link the colours and prevent holes appearing in the knitting. Take care not to pull the colours at the back too tight as this will distort the knitting.

BACK (SWEATER AND CARDIGAN)

Using the smaller needles and MC cast on 126 sts and work in twisted rib as follows:

Row 1 (rs): p2, (k2, p2) to end.
Row 2 (ws): k2, (p2, k2) to end.
Row 3: as row 1.
Row 4: as row 2.
Row 5: p2, (tw2, p2) to end.
Row 6: as row 2.

Repeat these 6 rows until work measures 2½in/6cm, ending with a ws row. Change to the larger needles and begin working from chart at row 1 (bottom right) with a knit row, joining in colours as required to row 66 (sweater) or row 79 (cardigan). Place markers for armholes at each end of row. Cont straight from chart until row 135 is complete. Change to MC and purl 1 row. Cont in cabled rib as follows:**

Row 1 (rs): (p1, k4, p1), rep to end.
Row 2 (ws): (k1, p4, k1) rep to end.
Row 3: as row 1.
Row 4: as row 2.
Row 5: (p1, c4b, p1), rep to end.
Row 6: as row 2. **

Work measures 25in/63½cm.
Cardigan only: repeat these 6 rows until work measures 27in/68½cm, ending with a ws row.
Both styles: cast off loosely in rib, placing markers at 43rd and 84th sts for neck opening.

SWEATER FRONT

Work exactly as given for Back.

CARDIGAN FRONTS

Pocket linings: Using the larger needles and MC, cast on 27 sts and work 5in/13cm in st st, ending with a k row. Make two and leave sts on a spare needle.

Using the smaller needles and MC, cast on 62 sts and work in twisted rib as set out for back for 2½in/6cm, ending with a ws row and inc 1 st at centre of last row. 63 sts.

Change to the larger needles and beg working from left or right side of chart at row 1 with a knit row as follows, joining in colours as required:

Omit overlapping parts of central scroll and coat of arms, and work these sts in background colour instead (rows 4 to 20 and rows 70 to 80).

Left Front (row 1): Knit 43 sts from right side of chart then the 20 sts from crown chart.
Right Front (row 1): Knit the 20 sts from crown chart, then the 43 sts from left side of chart. Cont in this way, combining the two charts.

Work straight until row 33 is complete, ws facing.

Divide for pocket: patt 20 sts (for left front) or 16 sts (for right front), place next 27 sts onto a st holder, purl 27 sts of pocket lining,

patt to end. Cont straight in patt until row 135 is complete. Change to MC and purl 1 row, dec 1 st at side edge, 62 sts.

Cont in cable patt as for back rep from ** to ** until work measures 25in/63½cm, ending with a rs row (for left front) or a ws row (for right front).

Shape neck: keeping continuity of cable patt cast off 11 sts at beg of next row, patt to end, then dec 1 st at neck edge of every foll row to 43 sts. Cont in cable patt with no further shaping until front matches back to shoulder. Cast off loosely.

POCKET EDGINGS (CARDIGAN ONLY)

Replace the 27 sts from st holder onto the smaller needles and with rs facing and using MC, knit 1 row, dec 1 st at centre to 26 sts. Work in twisted rib as set out for back for 1½in/4cm. Cast off loosely in rib.

FRONT BANDS (CARDIGAN ONLY)

Buttonhole band: using the smaller needles and MC, rs facing, knit up 130 sts from left front edge (for man's cardigan) or right front edge (for womans cardigan). Work in twisted rib as set out for back, beg row 2, for 6 rows. Make first set of buttonholes:

Buttonhole row 1: rib 3, cast off 4 sts, (rib 16, cast off 4 sts) 6 times, rib 3.
Buttonhole row 2: work in rib, casting on 4 sts over those sts cast off on previous row.

Rib 10 rows more then repeat the 2 buttonhole rows. Work 6 rows in rib, cast off loosely in rib.

Button band: work 26 rows in twisted rib as above, omitting buttonholes.

SWEATER SLEEVES

The sleeves are worked in st st with bobble

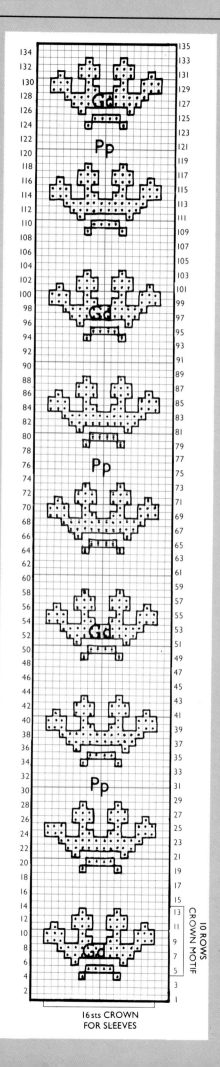

16 sts CROWN
FOR SLEEVES

10 ROWS CROWN MOTIF

SWEATER AND CARDIGAN – BACK AND FRONTS

RIGHT FRONT
43 sts + CROWN CHART

LEFT FRONT
43 sts + CROWN CHART

Gd	=	gold
Pp	=	purple
Rd	=	red
Em	=	emerald
Ct	=	claret
Bl	=	blue
Mg	=	mid grey

motifs worked in contrast colour and placed irregularly, according to the instructions below. The following colour combinations are recommended:

Main colour	Bobble colour
Gold	Purple
Purple	Emerald
Claret	Gold
Slate	Emerald or Blue

Bobble motif: each consists of 3 bobbles: a pair of bobbles worked on one knit row, and the third bobble worked on the foll knit row between the two. Each motif is worked with a separate length of contrast col. Leave the ends 2½in/6cm long and push them through to the rs for decoration.

To make bobble (mb): in contrast col, knit into front, back, front, back and front of next st, 5 contrast loops on needle. Pass 2nd, 3rd, 4th and 5th loops over the 1st, replace rem contrast st onto left hand needle and k in MC. Using the smaller needles and MC, cast on 42 sts and work in twisted rib as set out for Back for 2in/5cm, ending with a ws row.

Change to the larger needles and cont in st st, shaping sleeve by inc 1 st at each end of every row until there are 60 sts. Purl 1 row. Place first bobble motif as follows, joining in contrast col for the first bobble of the pair:

Next row: inc in first st, k39, mb, k1, mb, k to last st, inc in this st. Purl next row.

Next row: inc in first st, k41, mb, k to last st, inc in this st. (1 motif completed.)

Purl next row. Cont to shape sleeve by inc 1 st at both ends of every foll knit row throughout, and place motifs on knit rows as follows, using a separate length of yarn for each one:

Place second motif on 21st and 23rd sts of next row. Complete motif on next 2 rows, cont inc to 76 sts, ending with ws row. Start next motif on 12th st of next row, complete on next 2 rows, start next motif on 39th st of foll rs row. Complete motif and cont inc to 90 sts, ending with a ws row. Start motif on 70th st of next row, complete on next 2 rows, start next motif on 16th st of foll rs row. Complete on next 2 rows, start next motif on 46th st of foll rs row. Complete motif and cont to inc to 110 sts, ending with a ws row. Start motifs on 34th st of next row, and 72nd st of foll rs row. Complete this motif, 116 sts on needle. Now cont without shaping.

Work 5 rows, ending with a ws row, then start 2 motifs on 19th and 94th sts of next row. Complete motifs and work 7 rows, ending with ws row, start motif on 49th st of foll row. Complete this motif and work 7 rows, ending with ws row, start next motif on 81st st of next row. Complete motif, start last motif on 28th st of next rs row. Complete motif and cont in st st until sleeve measures 18in/46cm. Cast off loosely.

CARDIGAN SLEEVES

The sleeves are worked in st st with contrast crown motifs worked from the chart and placed according to the instructions. Work each crown with a separate ball of yarn, stranding MC loosely at the back of work, and weaving it in every 3rd st where necessary.

For recommended colour combinations, see sweater sleeves.

Using the smaller needles and MC, cast on 42 sts and work in twisted rib as for back for 2in/5cm, ending with a ws row. Change to the larger needles and beg with a k row proceed in st st, **shaping sleeve** as follows: inc 1 st at each end of first and every row to 58 sts, then inc 1 st at each end of every purl row until there are 116 sts. At the same time, place crown motifs as follows, starting on 5th row of sleeve:

Row 5: inc in first st, k16, patt 16 sts from row 1 of crown, k16, inc in last st.

Cont working crown from chart, shaping as above, until 10 rows of crown are complete. 62 sts. Cont shaping until there are 74 sts, ending with a ws row.

Next row: k11, patt 16 sts for crown, k20, patt 16 sts for crown, k11. Complete 2 crowns as set, still inc as before. Cont in st st, inc to 94 sts, ending with a ws row.

Next row: k3, patt 16 sts for crown, *k20, patt 16 sts for crown*, rep from * to *, k3. Complete 3 crowns as set, still inc as before and cont in st st, inc to 114 sts.

Next row: k31, patt 16 sts for crown, k20, patt 16 sts for crown, k31. Inc 1 st at each end of next row, 116 sts. Complete the 2 crowns with no further shaping. Work 10 rows st st.

Next row: k14, patt 16 sts for crown, *k20, patt 16 sts for crown*, rep from * to *, k14. Complete the 3 crowns, then cont in st st in MC only until sleeve measures 19in/48½cm. Cast off loosely.

COLLAR (BOTH STYLES)

Knitted using the smaller needles for cardigan, but the larger needles for sweater. Using MC, cast on 162 sts and work in cabled rib as given for back from ** to **. Repeat the 6 rows until collar measures 5½in/14cm. Cast off loosely in rib.

FINISHING

Darn in all loose ends carefully (except bobble motifs) closing all gaps and working up and down and not across the back of the work. Lightly steam press pieces avoiding all cabled sections.

Using backstitch, join shoulder seams. Using markers as a guide, join sleeves to body and join side and sleeve seams.

Sweater: oversew collar seam to make circle. With ws of collar to rs of neckline, and using a flat seam, oversew collar from inside of neckline with seam at centre back.

Cardigan: turn front bands in half to the inside and slip stitch in place. Sew round buttonholes and sew on buttons to correspond. Catch down pocket bands and slip stitch pocket linings in position. Using a flat oversewn seam, and with ws of collar to rs of neck edge, join collar to body, starting and finishing halfway across top of front bands.

SHIELD SWEATER AND CARDIGAN

These oversize garments are knitted in stocking stitch and reverse stocking stitch. Both sweater and cardigan are knitted from the same charts. The sweater has the large shield motif on the front, the cardigan features the same motif, but on the back. The sweater has small shield motifs worked in stocking stitch on a background of reverse stocking stitch on the back, and these are also knitted on the cardigan fronts. Both styles have small shield motifs on the sleeves. An embroidered motto is added to the scroll beneath the large shield after knitting. A completely different effect is achieved by using either bright contrasts or pastel colours.

SIZES
One large size to fit up to 40in/102cm bust/chest. For smaller size see tension paragraph.
Knitted measurements: width at underarm 30in/76cm; sleeve length 17in/43cm; length 24in/61cm (sweater), 26in/66cm (cardigan).

ABBREVIATIONS
See page 15.

MATERIALS
○ Both versions: use 6 colours of Rowan's Sandy Black Wool Twist
    Main colour (MC) Stone, Mid Grey, Slate Grey or Claret
    with 1 × 50g ball in each of 5 contrast colours: Gold (Gd), Blue (Bl), Purple (Pp), Red (Rd), Emerald (Em), OR Eau de Nil (N), Lilac (L), Rose (Rs), Mid Grey (Mg), Purple (Pp)
○ Sweater: 15 balls in main colour
○ Cardigan: 18 balls in main colour
○ 7 buttons for cardigan
○ 2 pairs of needles are required, one pair for main parts in the size to give the correct tension; one pair 4 sizes smaller for edgings
○ cable needle
○ large-eyed yarn needle

TENSION
Measured over rev st st pattern 18 sts and 24 rows to 4in/10cm using 5½mm (UK size 5) needles. Recommended needles for edgings 3¾mm (UK size 9).
To avoid disappointment, it is essential to check your tension carefully before commencing the garment and use the needles which give **you** the correct tension. **This may not be the size quoted in the standard tension**, as individual knitters vary.
How to check tension: using the recommended needles and MC, cast on 30 sts and work in rev st st for 8 rows.
Row 9: p15, k1, p14.

Row 10: k13, p3, k to end.
Row 11: p13, k5, p to end.
Row 12: k11, p7, k to end.
Row 13: p11, k9, p to end.
Row 14: k9, p11, k to end.
Row 15: p10, k11, p to end.
Rows 16 to 21: rep rows 14 and 15 three times.
Row 22: as row 14.
Row 23: k to end.
Cont in rev st st for 10 more rows. Cast off loosely. Lightly steam press the piece under a damp cloth. Pin the square down flat without stretching. Place a pin between 2 sts near the left, count 18 sts and mark with another pin between the 18th and 19th sts. Mark out 24 rows in the same way. Measure the distance

between the pins. This should be 4in/10cm in both directions. If it is less, your knitting is too tight – try one size larger needle; if it is more, your knitting is too loose – try one size smaller needle. Do not be afraid to go up or down more than one needle size. Repeat the process until the correct tension is obtained. Adjust the size of the second pair of needles accordingly.

Size note: if desired, a smaller size can be simply knitted from the same pattern by obtaining the needle size for the correct tension as above, and then adjusting both pairs of needles to one size smaller throughout. This should result in a garment approx 4in/10cm narrower **all round**, and approx 1½in/4cm shorter. Sweater on p. 84 is full size, and on p. 83 is smaller size.

NOTES ON WORKING PATTERN

One square of chart represents one stitch. Odd numbered rows are right side rows – read from right to left. Even numbered rows are wrong side rows – read from left to right. Each square is knit **or** purl as follows: all outlined pattern areas are worked in st st (odd rows knit, even rows purl). All background areas are worked in reverse st st (odd rows purl, even rows knit). The main shield and scroll are worked in st st in colours indicated. The small shields are worked in st st in MC with motif in contrast colour. Use separate balls of yarn for each area of colour, and avoid stranding colours at the back. Cross yarns when changing colour to link the colours and prevent holes appearing in the knitting. Use a separate ball of background colour at each side of the main shield.

Note: to give neat outlines around coloured areas: When contrast coloured plain stitches are replaced by background colour purl stitches on the next row, work these background colour stitches knit instead of purl, or vice versa. This avoids unwanted strands of contrast colour appearing on the rs. (This applies in particular around the scroll and crown shapes.)

SWEATER FRONT or CARDIGAN BACK

Using the smaller needles and MC, cast on 134 sts and work in twisted rib as follows:
Row 1(rs): p2, (k2, p2) to end.
Row 2(ws): k2, (p2, k2) to end.
Rows 3 and 4: rep rows 1 and 2.
Row 5: p2, (tw2, p2) to end.
Row 6: as row 2.
Rep rows 1 to 6 until work measures 2½in/6cm, ending with a ws row, increasing 1 st in last row. 135 sts.*
Change to the larger needles and begin working from chart (A) at bottom right with a purl row. Cont working from chart in rev st st, working scroll and shield in st st and joining colours as required as follows:
Row 1(rs): purl to end.

Row 2(ws): knit to end.
Rows 3 and 4: as rows 1 and 2.
Row 5: p36MC, k2Pp, p56MC, k2Pp, p to end in MC.
Row 6: k20MC, p1Em, k17MC, p3Em, p1Pp, k54MC, p1Pp, p3Em, k17MC, p1Em, k to end in MC.
Cont working from chart in this manner and beg small shields on even (ws) rows as marked. Cont until row 70 (sweater) OR row 76 (cardigan) is complete.
Shape armholes: keeping continuity of patt, cast off 9 sts at beg of next 2 rows, 117 sts. Cont working from chart until row 120 (sweater) OR row 122 (cardigan) is complete, noting centre of crown is longer for cardigan.**
Begin cable yoke as follows:
Row 1: p3, (k4, p2) to end.
Row 2: k2, (p4, k2) to last st, k1.
Rows 3 and 4: rep rows 1 and 2.
Row 5: p3, (c4b, p2) to end.
Row 6: as row 2.

Repeating rows 1 to 6, cont in cable rib until work measures 24in/61cm (sweater), 26in/66cm (cardigan) from beg. Cast off loosely in rib, placing markers for neck at 25th and 92nd sts (sweater).

SWEATER BACK

Work as given for front to *. Change to the larger needles and beg working from chart (B) at bottom right hand corner. Beg each shield motif on an even (ws) row, joining in colours as required until row 120 is complete. Now work cable rib as given for front until work matches front. Cast off loosely in rib, placing markers as front.

CARDIGAN FRONTS

Pocket linings: Using the larger needles and MC, cast on 26 sts and work 5in/13cm in rev st st ending with a knit row. Make two and leave on st holders.
Using the smaller needles and MC, cast on 66 sts and work in twisted rib as set out for back

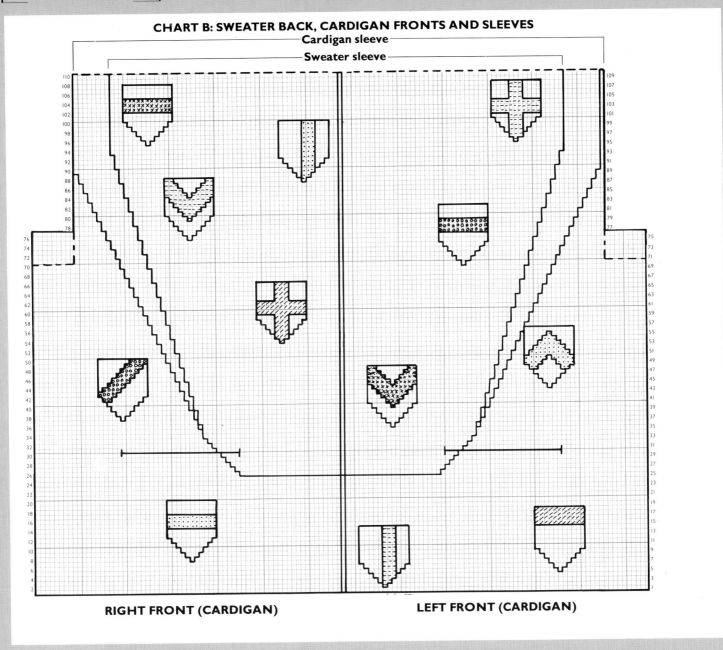

⊠ Em = emerald
⊡ Pp = Purple
⊿ Bl = blue
⊡ Gd = gold
⊟ Rd = red
  MC = main colour
  — — — = sweater shaping
  ———— = cardigan shaping

CHART B: SWEATER BACK, CARDIGAN FRONTS AND SLEEVES

Cardigan sleeve
Sweater sleeve

RIGHT FRONT (CARDIGAN)   **LEFT FRONT (CARDIGAN)**

for 2½in/6cm, ending with a ws row, increasing 1 st in last row. 67 sts. Change to the larger needles and rev st st and begin working from appropriate half of chart for left or right front at row 1 (bottom right). Cont working from chart beg each shield on an even (ws) row as marked, until row 30 is complete. Place pocket as follows:

Next row: p19 (left front) or p22 (right front), place next 26 sts onto st holder, p26 sts from pocket lining, p to end. Cont from chart until row 76 (left front) or row 77 (right front) is complete.

Shape armhole:

Next row: Cast off 9 sts, patt to end (58 sts). Cont working straight until row 110 of chart is complete. Work 12 rows rev st st.

Begin cable yoke and shape neck:
Row 1: p3, (k4, p2) to last st, p1.
Row 2: k3, (p4, k2) to last st, k1.
Rows 3 and 4: rep rows 1 and 2.
Row 5: p3, (c4b, p2) to last st, p1.
Row 6: as row 2.

Rep these 6 rows for cable patt. Cont in cable rib as set, cabling every 6th row until work measures 24½in/62cm, ending at centre front.

Next row: Cast off 11 sts, patt to end. Keeping continuity of cable rib, dec 1 st at

neck edge of every row until 38 sts rem. Cast off loosely in rib.

POCKET EDGINGS
Place 26 sts from st holder onto the smaller needles and using MC, with rs facing, work in twisted rib for 1½in/4cm as set out for back. Cast off in rib.

FRONT BANDS (CARDIGAN ONLY)
Left front: using MC and smaller needles, rs facing, knit up 122 sts and work 26 rows (2½in/6cm) in twisted rib as for back. Cast off loosely in rib.

Right front: work as left band, for 6 rows. Make first set of buttonholes as follows:
1st buttonhole row: patt 4 sts, (cast off 4 sts, patt 14) 6 times, cast off 4 sts, patt 6 sts.
2nd buttonhole row: work in patt, casting on 4 sts over sts cast off in previous row. Work 10 rows more, then rep buttonhole rows as above. Work 6 rows. Cast off loosely in rib.

SLEEVES (BOTH STYLES)

Using the smaller needles and MC, cast on 42 sts and work in twisted rib for 2in/5cm as set out for back, ending with a ws row, inc 1 st at beg and end of last row. 44 sts. Change to the larger needles and begin working from chart for sleeve, starting at row 1 with a purl row. Shape sleeve, keeping continuity of patt, by inc 1 st at each end of every foll row to 60 sts.
Cardigan only: inc 1 st each end of every foll alt row to 116 sts.
Sweater only: inc 1 st at each end of every foll 3rd row to 100 sts.
Both styles: cont working straight until chart is completed and cont until sleeve measures 17in/43cm. Cast off loosely.

COLLAR (BOTH STYLES)

Knitted using the smaller needles for cardigan, but the larger needles for sweater. Using MC cast on 162 sts.
Row 1(rs): (p1, k4, p1) to end.
Row 2(ws): (k1, p4, k1) to end.
Rows 3 and 4: rep rows 1 and 2.
Row 5: (p1, c4b, p1) to end.
Row 6: as row 2.
Rep rows 1 to 6 five more times or until collar measures 5in/13cm. Cast off loosely in rib.

FINISHING AND EMBROIDERY

Draw the lettering onto vanishing muslin or similar thin fabric or interlining using chart as guide. Securely pin the fabric lettering guide onto the knitting, positioning the lettering centrally on the scroll below main shield. Using a contrast colour (stone or gold are very good), stitch over the outlined letters and through the knitted fabric, using a large backstitch and following the outlines exactly as drawn. When completed, tear off the fabric guide to leave the stitching intact. Alternatively make up your own personal motto.

Carefully darn in all loose ends, working up and down, not across the work.
Lightly steam press pieces under a damp cloth, avoiding cabled edgings. Using backstitch, join shoulder seams. Join sleeves to body, setting corner of sleeve **squarely** into armhole by fitting sleeve to inner corner of cast off sts. Sew cast-off sts at underarm to top of sleeve seam at each side. Join side and rem seams.
Sweater only: using a flat seam, join collar into a circle. With ws of collar to rs of neckline pin collar in position and join to body with a flat edge to edge seam.
Cardigan only: turn front bands in half to inside, and slip stitch in place. Sew round buttonholes and sew on buttons to correspond. Catch down pocket bands and slip stitch pocket linings in position. Using a flat oversewn seam with ws of collar to rs of neck edge, join collar to body, starting and finishing halfway across top of front bands.

MAN'S VERSION OF SWEATER

Work as woman's sweater with the following exceptions:

BACK

Work exactly as for woman's version until cable yoke is complete. Do not cast off. Work a further 12 rows in cable yoke patt. 117 sts.
Shape shoulders: cast off 9 sts at beg of next 4 rows, then cast off 10 sts at beg of foll 4 rows. Cast off rem 41 sts.

FRONT

Work exactly as for woman's version until cable yoke is complete. Do not cast off.
Shape front neck: patt 48, turn and replace rem 69 sts on stitch holder.
Cont on these 48 sts and dec 1 st at neck edge of next 10 rows. Work 1 more row so that rs of work is facing. 38 sts.
Shape shoulders: cast off 9 sts at beg of next and foll alt row, work 1 row. Now cast off 10 sts at beg of next and foll alt row.
Replace sts from holder back onto needle. With rs facing rejoin yarn and cast off centre 21 sts. Complete to match first side.

SLEEVES

Work exactly as for woman's version until chart is completed. Now cont in rev st st until sleeve measures 19in/48cm. Cast off loosely.

COLLAR

Using the larger needles and MC cast on 114 sts.
Rep 6 rows as for woman's collar for 4½in/11½cm. Cast off loosely.

FINISHING

Join shoulder seams, using a backstitch. Placing open ends of collar to centre front and with ws of collar to rs of neckline, pin collar in position and join to body with a flat edge to edge seam.

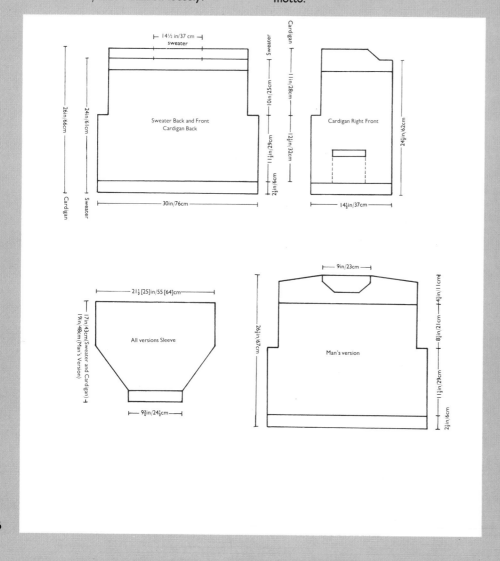

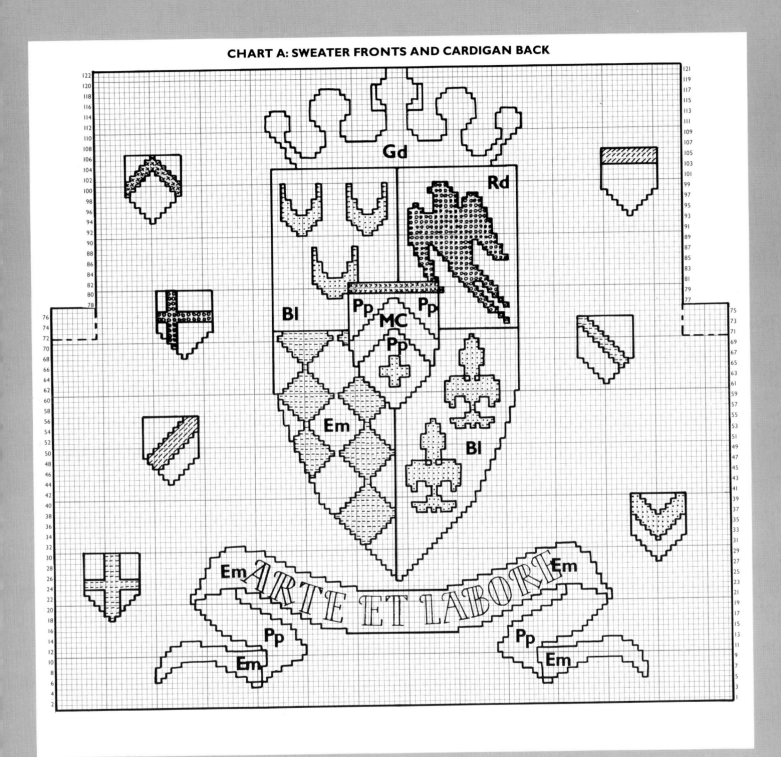

CHART A: SWEATER FRONTS AND CARDIGAN BACK

⊠ Em = emerald
⊡ Pp = Purple
⊿ Bl = blue
⊡ Gd = gold
⊟ Rd = red
MC = main colour
_ _ _ _ _ = sweater shaping
_____ = cardigan shaping

FLEUR DE LYS

This sweater is knitted in a combination of fairisle and block knitting from charts. For best results, be sure to follow the method of working given, and strand the yarns very loosely.

SIZE

One size to fit up to 38in/97cm bust.
Knitted measurements: width at underarm 25in/63cm; length 26in/66cm; sleeve length 20in/51cm.

ABBREVIATIONS

See page 15.

MATERIALS

○ 19 × 50g balls of Rowan's Sandy Black Wool

Twist in colours as follows:
  9 balls first colour (A)
  7 balls second colour (B)
  I ball each of three more colours for the fleur de lys motifs (1, 2, 3)
○ 2 pairs of needles are required, one pair for main parts in the size to give the correct tension; one pair 4 sizes smaller for edgings
○ stitch holder

TENSION

19 sts and 20 rows to 4in/10cm using 6mm (UK size 4) needles measured over fairisle pattern. Recommended needles for edgings: 4mm (UK size 8).

How to check tension: Read Notes on working pattern. Using the recommended needles and MC, cast on 31 sts. Start working from chart below at row 1 beginning at st 1 with a knit row, as follows. Work from sts 1–31 on k rows, and 31–1 on purl rows. Cont for 37 rows joining the colours as required. Cast off loosely. Pin the square down flat without stretching. Place a pin between 2 sts near the left, count 19 sts and mark with another pin between the 19th and 20th sts. Mark out 20 rows in the same way. Measure the distance between pins. This should be 4in/10cm in both directions. If it is less your knitting is too tight – try one size large needle. If it is more, your knitting is too loose – try one size smaller needle. Repeat the process until the correct tension is achieved. Do not be afraid to go up or down more than one needle size. Adjust the size of the second pair of needles accordingly.

BACK AND FRONT

SLEEVES

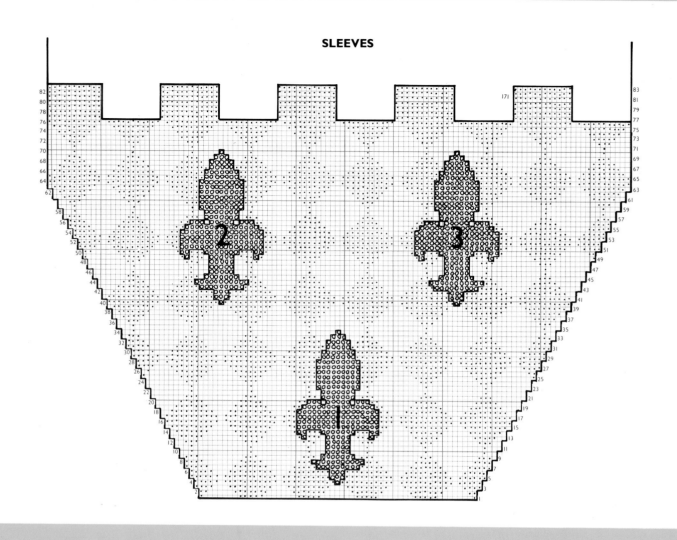

NOTES ON WORKING PATTERN

One square of the chart represents one stitch. Odd numbered rows (rs) are knit – read from right to left; even numbered rows (ws) are purl – read from left to right. When working fairisle, weave colour not in use **loosely** behind every 4th stitch and cross the yarns when changing colour to link the colours and prevent holes appearing in the knitting. Join in separate lengths of yarn for each fleur de lys motif and for background colours between motifs. Do not strand contrast colours behind fleur de lys motifs. Take care not to pull the colours at the back too tight as this will distort the knitting.

BACK AND FRONT

Using the smaller needles and A cast on 120 sts and work diagonal rib as follows:
Row 1(rs): (k3, p3) to end.
Row 2(ws): (k2, p3, k1) to end.
Row 3: (p2, k3, p1) to end.
Row 4: (p3, k3) to end.
Row 5: (k1, p3, k2) to end.
Row 6: (p1, k3, p2) to end.
Work rows 1 to 6 twice more.
Change to the larger needles and start working from chart at row 1 with a knit row, joining in colours where required. Work straight from chart until row 58 is complete.

Shape armholes: cast off 10 sts at beg of next 2 rows.* 100 sts.
Work straight from chart until row 106 is complete.
Change to the smaller needles and work 3in/7½cm of diagonal rib as set out for bottom edge. Cast off loosely in rib, placing markers for neck at 30th and 78th sts.

SLEEVES

Using the smaller needles and A, cast on 54 sts and work diagonal rib as for back, repeat rows 1 to 6 twice, inc 3 sts evenly on last row. 57 sts. Start working from chart at row 1 with a knit row, joining in colours as required.
Shape sleeves: inc 1 st at each end of 2nd and every foll alt row to 119 sts.
Cont straight from chart until row 83 is complete. Change to the smaller needles and using B only, continue in st st from chart until sleeve measures 21in/51cm.

FINISHING

Lightly steam press pieces under a damp cloth, avoiding edgings. Using backstitch, join shoulder seams. Set in sleeves, fitting them squarely into armhole so that corner of sleeves fits into inner corner of armhole. Join underarms to top of sleeve at each side. Join remaining sleeve seams. Darn in all loose ends.

⊡	= A
▢	= B
◎	= 1, 2 or 3

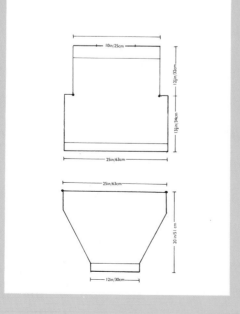

SMALL SHIELDS

This simple sweater with slash neck looks good on both men and women. It has an overall design of shields knitted in stocking stitch with yoke and edgings in diagonal rib. Have fun with the colours – you can choose a brightly coloured background, and substitute a dark colour in the shields instead.

SIZE
The same basic size fits a woman up to 38in/97cm bust loosely OR a man up to 40in/102cm chest.
Knitted measurements: back width at underarm 24in/60cm; length 24 [26½]in/ 61 [67]cm; sleeve length 18 [20½]in/46 [52]cm.
Size note: a smaller size can be obtained by just changing the needle size. First obtain the correct tension (see below), then use 1 size smaller needles. The difference in size will be approx 5in/12½cm all round narrower and 1½in/3½cm shorter.

ABBREVIATIONS
See page 15.

MATERIALS
○ 20 [21] × 50g balls of Rowan's Sandy Black Wool Twist in colours as follows:
10 [11] balls in main colour (MC), mid grey, slate grey, claret or stone
2 balls each of 5 colours for shields: red (R) (or slate grey if MC is red); emerald (E); purple (P); blue (B); gold (G)
○ 2 pairs of needles are required, one pair in the size to give the correct tension; one pair 3 sizes smaller for edgings.

TENSION
Measured over fairisle pattern, 21 sts and 22 rows to 4in/10cm using 5mm (UK size 6) needles or the size to give correct tension. Recommended needles for edging 3¾mm (UK size 9).
To avoid disappointment, it is essential to check your tension carefully before commencing the garment and use the needles which give **you** the correct tension. **This may not be the size quoted in the standard tension** as individual knitters vary.
How to check tension: Read paragraph Notes on working pattern. Using the recommended needles and MC, cast on 30 sts. Begin working from the chart below at row 1 and cont in st st, until row 30 is complete. Cast off. Pin the square down flat without stretching. Place a pin between 2 sts near the left, count 21 sts and mark with another pin between the 21st and 22nd sts. Mark out 22 rows in the same way. Measure the distance between the pins. This should be 4in/10cm in both directions. If it is less, your knitting is too tight – use one size larger needle. If it is more, your knitting is too loose – try one size

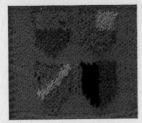

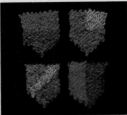

smaller needle. Repeat the process until the correct tension is achieved, and do not be afraid to go up or down more than one needle size. Adjust the size of the second pair of needles accordingly. As an additional check, 2 shields measure 3¾in/9½cm wide and 4½in/11½cm deep.

NOTES ON WORKING PATTERN
One square of chart represents one stitch. Odd numbered rows (rs) are knit – read from right to left; even numbered rows (ws) are purl – read from left to right. Use one ball of MC across the rows but use separate lengths of colour for each shield. Cross the yarns when changing colour to link the colours and prevent holes appearing in the knitting. To minimize tangling of colours, wind small bobbins (which can be made from card) of each colour, and allow these to hang close to the needle, just unravelling a small amount at a time when required. Weave in MC when not in use loosely behind shields every 3rd st.

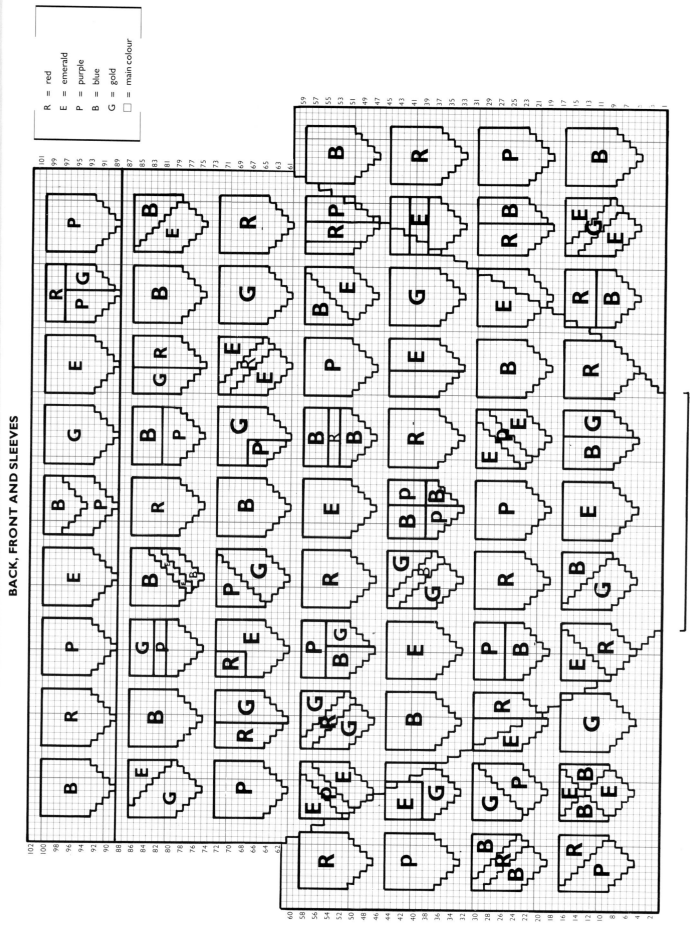

BACK, FRONT AND SLEEVES

R = red
E = emerald
P = purple
B = blue
G = gold
□ = main colour

SLEEVES: 37 sts

BACK AND FRONT

Using the smaller needles and MC, cast on 126 sts and work diagonal rib as follows:

Row 1(rs): (k3, p3) to end.
Row 2(ws): (k2, p3, k1) to end.
Row 3: (p2, k3, p1) to end.
Row 4: (p3, k3) to end.
Row 5: (k1, p3, k2) to end.
Row 6: (p1, k3, p2) to end.

Repeat rows 1 to 6 until edging measures 2½in/6cm, ending with a ws row and dec 1 st at end of last row. 125 sts.

Change to larger needles. Begin working from chart from row 1 at bottom right with a knit row. Cont in st st, joining in colours as required and taking care not to pull the yarn too tight across the back of work. Cont working from chart until row 60 is complete.

For man's version only: work one extra band of shields (14 rows) taken from the chart.

Shape armholes: cast off 10 sts at beg of next 2 rows. 105 sts. Cont working straight from chart until row 102 is complete.

Change to the smaller needles and cont in MC, in diagonal rib as follows:

Row 1(rs): (k3, p3) to last 3 sts, k3.
Row 2(ws): p2, k1, (k2, p3, k1) to end.
Row 3: (p2, k3, p1) to last 3 sts, p2, k1.
Row 4: k3, (p3, k3) to end.
Row 5: (k1, p3, k2) to last 3 sts, k1, p2.
Row 6: k1, p2, (p1, k3, p2) to end.

Repeat rows 1 to 6 as set until diagonal rib measures 3in/8cm. Cast off loosely, placing markers for neck opening at 28th and 78th sts.

SLEEVES

Using the smaller needles and MC, cast on 36 sts and work 2in/5cm of diagonal rib as set out for back, ending with a ws row. Inc 1 st at end of last row. 37 sts. Change to the larger needles and start working from chart for sleeve at row 1 with a knit row and cont in st

st, shaping sleeve as follows:

Inc 1 st at each end of next and every foll row to 53 sts. Inc 1 st at each end of every foll alt row to 105 sts. Cont straight from chart until row 88 is complete.

For man's version only: Work 1 extra band of shields here.

Cast off loosely.

FINISHING

Lightly steam press pieces, avoiding diagonal rib. Sew in all loose ends. Using back stitch seams throughout, join shoulder seams to markers. Set in sleeves making sure they are set in squarely to inner corner of armhole (A). Join underarm, side and sleeve seams.

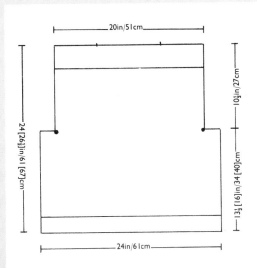

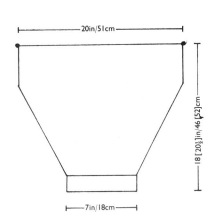

section 4
ORNAMENTAL

THE ORNAMENTAL DESIGNS ARE ALL DECOR-
ATED WITH ORNATE AND INTRICATE PAT-
TERNS, KNITTED IN RICH COLOURS, AND OFTEN
INCLUDING EMBROIDERED DETAILS. ANY OF
THESE DESIGNS WILL TURN HEADS WHEREVER
YOU WEAR THEM! I HAVE MADE SPECIAL USE
OF CONTRASTING YARN TEXTURES, PARTICU-
LARLY ROWAN'S SANDY BLACK WOOL TWIST
YARN COMBINED WITH LONG-HAIRED PURE
ANGORA TO HIGHLIGHT AREAS OR MOTIFS. THE
EFFECT IS DRAMATIC AND GIVES A STRONG
IMPACT WHILE USING THE MINIMAL QUANTITY
OF EXPENSIVE ANGORA.

THE STAINED GLASS SWEATER HAS ITS ORIGIN
IN THE BEAUTIFUL AND INTENSE COLOURINGS
TO BE SEEN IN STAINED GLASS WINDOWS EVERY-
WHERE. THE OUTLINED 'LEADING' EFFECT IN
THIS DESIGN ALSO EVOKES EARLY MEMORIES OF
MY FAMILY'S ASSOCIATIONS WITH THE MAKING
OF WINDOWS CALLED 'LEADED LIGHTS'.

THE OUTLINE FOR EACH 'PANE' IS EMBROID-
ERED ON AFTER THE KNITTING IS COMPLETED.
USE BLACK FOR A VERY POSITIVE LOOK, GREY
FOR A MORE SUBTLE EFFECT. THIS THEME
WORKS NOT ONLY WITH STRONG, VIBRATING
COLOURS, BUT ALSO WITH A PALE OR NEU-
TRAL PALETTE, IN WHICH CASE THE PATTERNS
LOOK SOFTER AND MORE REMINISCENT OF
PATCHWORK.

I HAVE USED NOT JUST THE IDEA BUT THE
TECHNIQUE OF PATCHWORK FOR THE NEXT
GROUP OF DESIGNS. THE GREAT ADVANTAGE OF
THIS METHOD OF WORKING IS THAT IT ENABLES
THE KNITTER TO CREATE QUITE COMPLEX PAT-
TERNING IN SMALL SECTIONS – AND MAKE A
GARMENT THAT WOULD BE TOO DAUNTING TO
KNIT IN ONE BIG PIECE. THE REPEATED PAT-
TERNS WORK WELL BECAUSE THE DESIGNS
THEMSELVES ARE BOLD AND COMPLEX. I HAVE
BASED THE JACKET AND COAT ON LARGE DIA-
MONDS AND THE GARMENTS ARE PLANNED ALL
IN ONE SO THE SEAMS BECOME PART OF THE
OVERALL DESIGN.

I LIKE TO LINE MY COATS AND JACKETS IN
HEAVY CRÊPE SATIN FABRIC IN STRONG COL-

OURS TO COMPLEMENT THE YARNS, WHICH
TRANSFORMS THEM INTO SUMPTUOUS EVENING
WEAR.

THE HIGHLY ORNAMENTAL LOTUS FLOWER
AND TAPESTRY FLOWER MOTIFS ARE USED TO
DECORATE THE STYLISH TUNIC AND SWEATER
SHAPES. LARGE SCALE PATTERNS POSITIONED
BOLDLY ON THE BODY CAN BE VERY FLATTER-
ING. THE MOTIF ITSELF CAN BE CHANGED QUITE
EASILY – JUST GRAPH OUT YOUR OWN DESIGN
TO FIT. IT LOOKS EQUALLY STUNNING KNITTED
PLAIN IN ONE OF THE PRIMARY WOOL TWIST
COLOURS.

THE ROSETTE DESIGN IS MY FAVOURITE IN THIS
SECTION, KNITTED IN PURE ANGORA ON A
BACKGROUND OF WOOL. USING ONE PLAIN
AND ONE TEXTURED YARN CREATES AN UN-
USUAL SURFACE, INTERESTING TO THE TOUCH
AS WELL AS THE EYE. THE BRIGHT CONTRASTS
IN THE CENTRE OF THE ROSETTES ADD TO THE
RICHNESS OF THE COLOURS AND CAN BE
EMBROIDERED AFTERWARDS TO MAKE THE
KNITTING EASIER.

FAIRGROUNDS ARE A FAVOURITE SOURCE OF
IDEAS – THE ORNATE DECORATIONS AND CON-
FUSION OF PATTERNS ARE SO EXCITING. ALL
THE FUN OF KNITTING IS HERE IN THE MERRY-
GOROUND COAT – CABLES, BOBBLES, FAIRISLE,
BLOCK KNITTING, EMBROIDERY, TASSELS,
FLOWERS – THE LOT! BUT EVERY ELEMENT IS
INTRODUCED QUITE CAREFULLY: THE CABLES
ARE EMBEDDED, NOT EMBOSSED, AND FADE
GRADUALLY INTO THE COLOUR PATTERNS. THE
ASYMMETRY OF THE DESIGN, WITH ITS PLAIN
AND PATTERNED AREAS ALSO OWES SOMETHING
TO THE IMAGES ON PLAYING CARDS WHICH
HAVE ALWAYS FASCINATED ME. EVEN THE
NECKBAND OF THE SWEATER SHOWN HERE IS
PART OF THE PATTERN. I HAVE CHOSEN PURE
ANGORA YARN FOR THE EVENING COAT,
MAKING IT MORE SOPHISTICATED THAN THE
SWEATER, WHICH IS KNITTED IN MOHAIR.
HOWEVER, YOU COULD ALSO MAKE THE COAT
IN MOHAIR.

STAINED GLASS

This classic styled sweater is knitted in stocking stitch in a hexagonal patchwork pattern using 7 colours of Rowan's Sandy Black Wool Twist. The stained glass window effect is created by outlining each 'pane' with chain stitch embroidery after knitting, worked with a needle or a crochet hook in main colour to match the ribbed edgings. Try this sweater in pale colours for a more understated effect.

SIZES

There are 2 sizes to fit up to 38in/97cm or up to 42in/107cm bust/chest.

Knitted measurements: back width at underarm 21 [22¾]in/53 [58]cm; length 25¾ [26½]in/65½ [67]cm; sleeve length 26¼/66½cm.

ABBREVIATIONS

See page 15.

MATERIALS

○ 22 × 50g balls of Rowan's Sandy Black Wool Twist in colours as follows:
    4 balls in main colour (MC), Slate Grey
    4 balls in 1st contrast Purple (Pp)
    3 balls in each of 2nd, 3rd, 4th and 5th contrast colours; Blue (Bl), Claret (Ct), Gold (Gd), Emerald (Em)
    2 balls in 6th contrast colour Red (Rd)
○ 2 pairs of needles are required, one pair for main parts in the size to give the correct tension; one pair 2 sizes smaller for edgings
○ large-eyed yarn needle for making up and embroidery (or a medium crochet hook)

TENSION

Measured over honeycomb pattern, 19 sts and 25 rows to 4in/10cm using 5mm (UK size 6) needles or the size to give correct tension. Recommended needles for edging: 4mm (UK size 8).

To avoid disappointment, it is essential to check your tension carefully before commencing the garment and use the needles which give **you** the correct tension. **This may not be the size quoted in the standard tension,** as individual knitters vary.

How to check tension: using the recommended needles and 3 different colours, A, B, C, cast on 12 sts with each colour (36 sts) and work in vertical stripes of 12 sts each as follows:

Row 1: knit 12A, 12B, 12C.
Row 2: purl 12C, 12B, 12A.

Rep these 2 rows 15 times. Cast off.
Pin the square down flat without stretching. Place a pin between 2 sts near the left, count 19 sts and mark with another pin between the 19th and 20th sts. Mark out 25 rows in the same way. Measure the distance between pins. This should be 4in/10cm in both

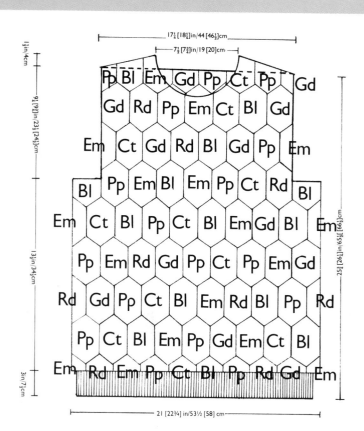

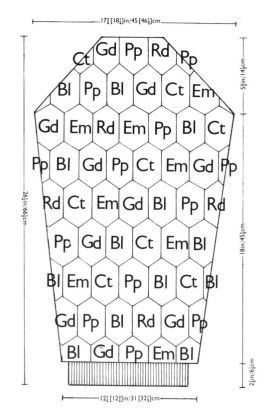

directions. If it is less your knitting is too tight – try one size larger needle. If it is more, your knitting is too loose – try one size smaller needle. Repeat the process until the correct tension is achieved. Do not be afraid to go up or down more than one needle size. Adjust the size of the second pair of needles accordingly.

NOTES ON WORKING PATTERN

Knitted in stocking stitch from the chart, each honeycomb shape is 12 sts wide and 22 rows deep. The colours are placed according to the key. When working from chart one square represents one stitch. Odd numbered rows (rs) are knit – read from right to left. Even numbered rows (ws) are purl – read from left to right. Use a separate ball or length of yarn for each coloured shape and cross the yarns when changing colour to link the colours and prevent holes appearing in the knitting. **Do not** strand or weave yarn across back of work. To minimize tangling of colours wind small bobbins (which can be made of card) of each colour and allow these to hang close to the needle, just unravelling a small amount at a time as needed.

BACK

Using the smaller needles and MC cast on 76 [80] sts. Work in k2, p2 rib for 3in/7½cm. On the last row inc in first and every 3rd st to 102 [108] sts. Change to the larger needles and using chart as a guide continue in honeycomb pattern as follows, breaking off and joining in yarns as required:
Row 1: knit 3 [6]Em, 12Gd, 12Rd, 12Pp, 12Bl, 12Ct, 12Pp, 12Em, 12Rd, 3 [6]Em.

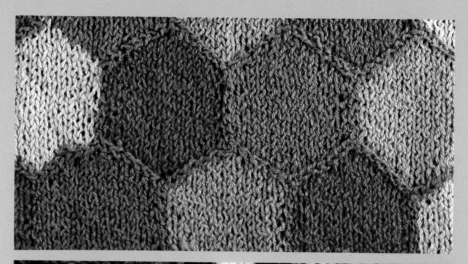

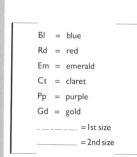

Bl = blue
Rd = red
Em = emerald
Ct = claret
Pp = purple
Gd = gold
– – – – – = 1st size
——— = 2nd size

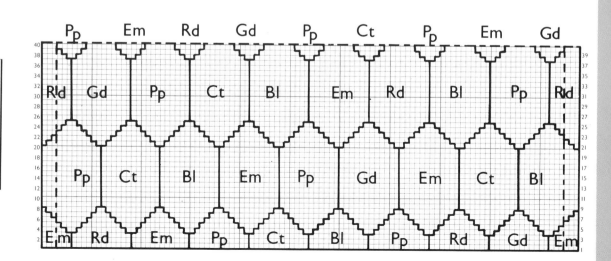

Row 2: purl 3 [6]Em, 12Rd, 12Em, 12Pp, 12Ct, 12Bl, 12Pp, 12Rd, 12Gd, 3 [6]Em.

Row 3: as row 1.

Row 4: purl 2 [5]Em, 2Pp, 10Rd, 2Ct, 10Em, 2Bl, 10Pp, 2Em, 10Ct, 2Pp, 10Bl, 2Gd, 10Pp, 2Em, 10Rd, 2Ct, 10Gd, 2Bl, 2 [5]Em.

Row 5: knit 1 [4]Em, 4Bl, 8Gd, 4Ct, 8Rd, 4Em, 8Pp, 4Gd, 8Bl, 4Pp, 8Ct, 4Em, 8Pp, 4Bl, 8Em, 4Ct, 8Rd, 4Pp, 1 [4]Em.

Row 6: purl 0 [3]Em, 6Pp, 6Rd, 6Ct, 6Em, 6Bl, 6Pp, 6Em, 6Ct, 6Pp, 6Bl, 6Gd, 6Pp, 6Em, 6Rd, 6Ct, 6Gd, 6Bl, 0 [3]Em.

Cont in patt as now set, breaking off and joining in colours as given on diagram until work measures 16½in/42cm from beg, ending with a purl row.

Shape armholes: keeping continuity of patt cast off 9 [10] sts at beg of next 2 rows. 84 [88] sts. (It is no longer necessary to introduce new colours at edge sts.)

Cont in patt with no further shaping until work measures 25½ [25¾]in/65 [66]cm from beg, ending with a purl row.

Shape shoulder: cast off 24 [25] sts loosely at beg of next 2 rows.

Leave rem 36 [38] sts on a stitch holder.

FRONT

Work as for back until work measures 23½ [23¾]in/59½ [61]cm from beg, ending with a purl row.

Divide for neck: patt 33 [34] sts, turn, leave rem sts on a stitch holder and cont in patt on first set of sts only as follows: keeping continuity of patt dec 1 st at neck edge on next 9 rows. 24 [25] sts. Work in patt with no further shaping until armhole measures same as back, ending on a purl row.

Shape shoulder: keeping continuity of patt cast off 3 sts at beg of next and foll 6 alt rows. Cast off rem 3 [4] sts.

Return to sts on stitch holder and slip next 18 [20] sts onto a length of yarn. Complete to correspond with first side of neck, reversing shapings.

SLEEVES

Using the smaller needles and MC, cast on 50 [52] sts. Work in k2, p2 rib for 2½in/6cm. On the last row inc in every 5th st to 60 [62] sts. Change to the larger needles and keeping patt correct during shaping beg working in patt as follows:

Row 1: knit 12 [13]Bl, 12Em, 12Pp, 12Gd, 12 [13]Bl.

Row 2: purl 12 [13]Bl, 12Gd, 12Pp, 12Em, 12 [13]Bl.

Row 3: as row 1.

Row 4: purl 1 [2]Gd, 10Bl, 2Pp, 10Em, 2Bl, 10Pp, 2Rd, 10Gd, 2Em, 10Bl, 1 [2]Pp.

Cont in patt as now set, inc 1 st at both ends of every 8th row until there are 86 [88] sts. Cont in patt with no further shaping until work measures 20½in/52cm from beg.

Shape top: keeping continuity of patt cast off 2 sts at beg of next 34 rows.

Cast off rem 18 [20] sts loosely.

NECKBAND

Using a backstitch seam join right shoulder. With rs facing, using MC, and smaller needles knit up approx 102 [106] sts evenly around neck edge, including sts on holder and length of yarn. Work 4in/10cm of k2, p2 rib.

Cast off loosely in rib.

FINISHING AND EMBROIDERY

Darn in all loose ends, closing any gaps and working up and down the knitting not across. Using either a large eyed needle or a crochet hook and MC, outline all coloured shapes with a line of chain stitch (around all honeycomb shapes) taking care not to pull embroidery too tight. Lightly steam press pieces. Using a backstitch seam join left shoulder and neckband seam. Set sleeve into armhole placing inner corner of sleeve to corner of armhole. Join first 1¾in/4½cm of sleeve seams to cast off sts at underarm at each side. Join side and rem sleeve seams. Fold neckband in half onto ws and slip stitch to inside taking care neckband fits over head.

Note: Woman's Stained Glass Jacket design is available as a kit – see p. 122.

PATCHWORK JACKET AND COAT

The jacket and coat are both constructed in the same way from a patchwork of diamonds and triangles – the coat simply requires more pieces. Each main piece is worked from the same chart in stocking stitch using a combination of two yarns. Two designs are illustrated – the Tapestry Flower design in wool and angora, and the Leaf and Lotus design in wool and chenille.

SIZE
One size to fit up to bust 40in/102cm.
Knitted measurements: all round width at underarm including edgings 60in/152cm; jacket length 28in/71cm; coat length 43in/109cm.
A smaller size can be achieved by changing needle size and tension (see below).

ABBREVIATIONS
See page 15.

TAPESTRY FLOWER DESIGN: MATERIALS
○ 14 or 19 × 50g balls of Rowan's Sandy Black Wool Twist in 4 colours as follows:

	Jacket	Coat
main colour (A)	9	12
1st contrast (leaf colour B)	3	4
2nd contrast (C)	1	2
3rd contrast (D)	1	1

○ 22 or 34 × 20g balls of 100% Angora in 3 colours as follows:

	Jacket	Coat
border colour (E)	18	28
1st flower colour (F)	2	3
2nd flower colour (G)	2	3

○ oddments of wool in 2 colours for embroidery
○ 1 pair of needles is required in the size to give correct tension
○ large eyed yarn needle
○ **Colourway 1:** A = Slate Grey, B = Emerald, C = Claret, D = Red, E = Grape, F = Burgundy, G = Fuchsia
○ **Colourway 2 (as shown on facing page):** A = Stone, B = Eau de nil, C = Mid-Grey, D = Rose, E = Grape, F = Cedar, G = Grape

TENSION
Measured over stocking stitch 18 sts and 24 rows to 4in/10cm, using 5½mm (UK size 5) needles, or the size to give the correct tension.
To avoid disappointment, it is essential to check your tension carefully before commencing the garment and use the needles which give **you** the correct tension. **This may not be the size quoted in the standard tension**, as individual knitters vary.
How to check tension: using the recommended needles and E, cast on 62 sts and work 4 rows garter stitch. Then beg

working from chart c at row 1 with a knit row (see Notes on working pattern). Cont in st st joining in colours as required, shaping as shown on chart until row 40 is complete. Pin triangle down flat without stretching and measure each side. The triangle should measure: base 13½in/34cm; height 6½in/17cm; side edge 9½in/24cm.

If the triangle is smaller your knitting is too tight — try one size larger needle. If the triangle is larger your knitting is too loose — try one size smaller needle. Repeat the process until the correct tension is achieved. Do not be afraid to go up or down more than one needle size. If the size is correct, this piece can be used as one of the garment pieces.

Size note: for a smaller size, follow tension instructions above to obtain correct tension, then use one size smaller needles. This should result in a garment approx 4in/10cm narrower and correspondingly shorter.

NOTES ON WORKING PATTERN

One square of chart represents one stitch. Odd numbered rows (rs) are knit – read from right to left, even numbered rows (ws) are purl – read from left to right. Shapings are worked by following the outline of chart, increasing or decreasing one stitch on the row where the outline moves in or out by one square. When working pattern from chart use a separate ball of yarn for each area of colour especially on either side of main motif. Do not strand yarn across back of work.

MAIN PIECE

Both garments are made up of the same basic diamonds and triangles, but used in different quantities – see below. The bottom edge of the jacket is straight but the coat is angled at the lower front edges. Knit the following pieces from the charts:

	Jacket	Coat
a =	19 pieces;	a = 26 pieces.
b =	2 pieces;	b = 4 pieces.
c =	6 pieces;	c = 6 pieces.
d =	2 pieces;	d = 1 piece.
e =	2 pieces.	e = 1 piece.

When working pieces from charts note any extra instructions that may be given for g st edgings on cuff pieces (c). Ensure that cast-on edge is loose on one piece c for back neck.

JACKET EDGINGS

The edgings are knitted in garter st: the front and neck edging is knitted separately and sewn on; the lower edging is knitted on after assembling the pieces.

Front edging: using E cast on 28sts and work straight in g st until band is approx 56in/142cm long. Leave sts on a holder.

COAT EDGING

This edging is knitted in a slipstitch honeycomb pattern and fits all round front, neck and lower edges of coat. The band is shaped to form a shawl collar. Using E cast on 29 sts and knit 1 row then work as follows:

Row 1 (rs): p1, (sl 3, p1) rep to end.
Rows 2 to 5: work in st st starting knit.
Row 6: k2, (k next st tog with strand of yarn below on p side, k3) rep to end, ending last rep k2.
Row 7: p3, (sl 3, p1) rep to last 2 sts, p2.
Rows 8 to 11: as rows 2 to 5.
Row 12: k4, (k next st tog with strand of yarn below on p side, k3) rep to end, ending last rep k4.
These 12 rows form the patt. Cont in patt until work measures 34in/86cm.
Shape collar: keeping continuity of patt, inc 1 st at each end of the next and every foll 6th row until there are 57 sts. Work straight until edging measures 57in/145cm from beg. Dec 1 st at each end of next and every foll 6th row until 29 sts rem. Cont straight for a further 60in/152cm. Leave sts on a holder.

FINISHING

Position pieces as in the layout diagram, taking care to follow the direction of the arrows. Use one of the following methods of

LAYOUT DIAGRAM

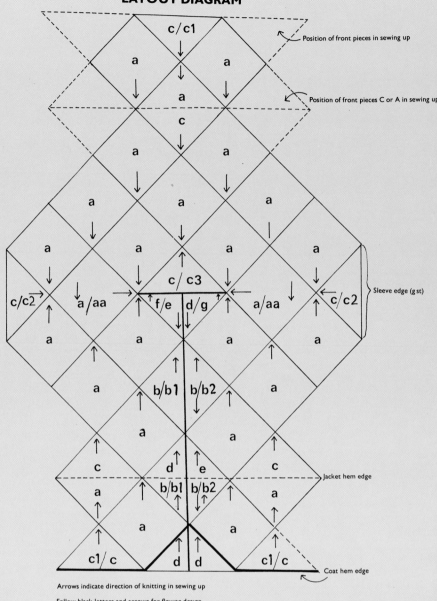

Arrows indicate direction of knitting in sewing up

Follow black letters and arrows for flower design

Follow green letters and arrows for leaf design where these are given

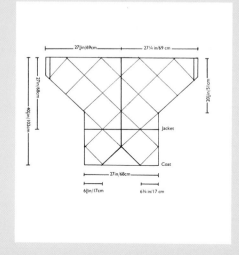

CHART aa

LEAF AND LOTUS DESIGN

b1, b2, c1, c2, c3, d, e, f, g: for triangles, subdivide diamond charts as shown, ignoring central motif.
Note: c3 = c2, but reverse colours.

CHART a

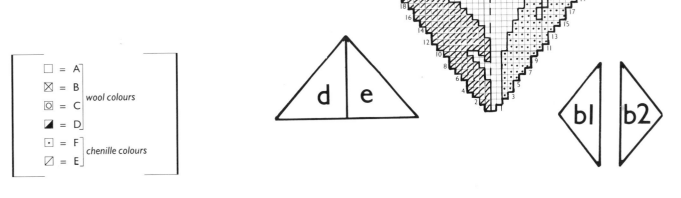

c1

c2 (c3)

f   g

d   e

b1   b2

	= A	
⊠	= B	*wool colours*
⊙	= C	
◨	= D	
·	= F	*chenille colours*
◪	= E	

103

TAPESTRY FLOWER DESIGN

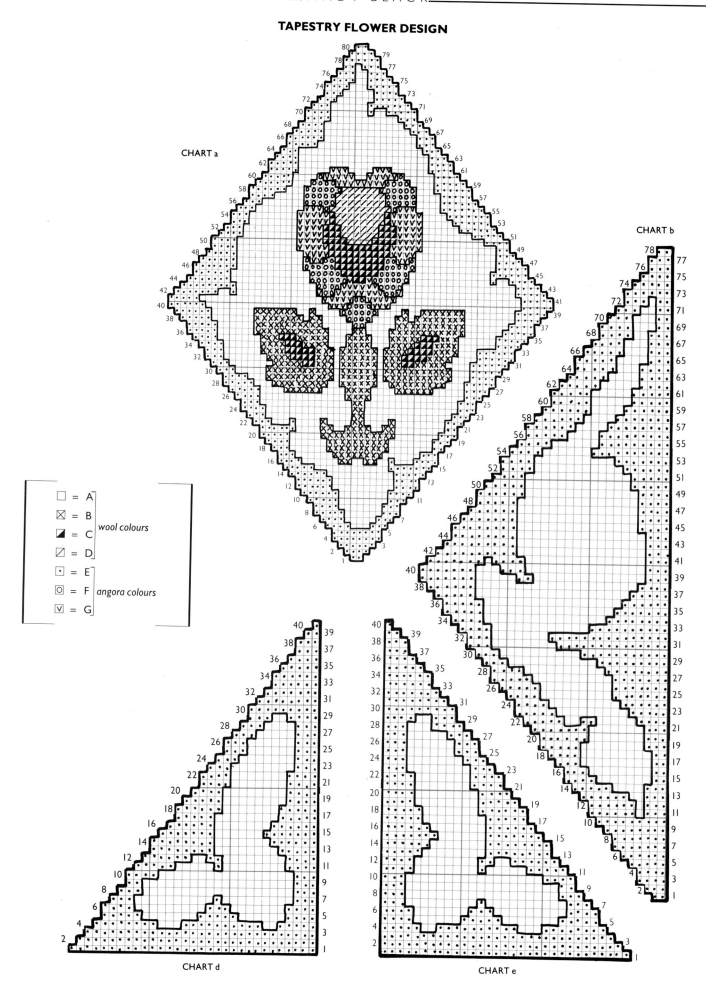

CHART a

CHART b

= A

= B

= C   *wool colours*

= D

= E

= F   *angora colours*

= G

CHART d

CHART e

joining pieces as preferred. Note that to complete the sides, pieces from the front join into the back filling in areas marked by dotted lines. Join sleeve seams (2 diamonds).

Method 1: With rs tog, and taking very narrow seams, backstitch the pieces together.

Method 2: Using a medium crochet hook, and working from the rs, ie with ws of pieces tog, join the seams with a row of double crochet, taking care to work evenly along all sides. This results in an attractive ridge on the right side.

Back neck: although it appears there is no allowance for back neck, in reality, provided that the cast on edge is not too tight, the width of the back neck piece is sufficient to allow the front pieces d and e (or f and g) to be joined to back piece c and leave a 3½in/9cm gap between front edges.

Jacket edging: using E and with rs facing, knit up 240 sts along bottom edge and work 1½in/4cm in g st. Cast off. Starting with cast-on edge, pin front band in place, stretching slightly to fit up one front, across gap for neck and down other front. Adjust the length of band to fit exactly by unravelling or knitting extra length. Cast off. Backstitch in position, fold in half to inside and slip stitch in place. Neaten bottom edges.

Coat edging: with rs tog, place centre of collar to centre back and pin edging all round front and bottom edges, easing around shaped front edge and slightly stretching across the back, until the two ends meet at the side. Adjust the length of the band to fit exactly by unravelling or knitting extra length. Backstitch edging in position, join the seam, turn to inside and slipstitch in place.

Embroidery: using oddments of 2 contrast colours alternately, work a curved line of 5 or 7 French knots in centre of each flower following the line between the upper and lower sections of the centre.

LEAF AND LOTUS DESIGN

This version is worked exactly as the Tapestry Flower design, but following the charts for leaf and lotus pattern instead. The total number of pieces of jacket and coat versions, tension and all other details are the same, but the layout varies slightly because the design is not symmetrical. There is no embroidery on this version.

MATERIALS

○ 10 or 20 × 50g balls of Rowan's Sandy Black Wool Twist in 4 colours as follows:

	Jacket	Coat
main colour (A) Stone	10	13
1st contrast (B) Purple	2	3
2nd contrast (C) Claret	1	2
3rd contrast (D) Red	1	1

○ 12 × 50g balls of Rowan Fine Chenille in 2 colours as follows:

edging and 1st leaf colour (E) Steel	6	11
2nd leaf colour (F) Turquoise	2	3

○ 2 pairs of needles are required, one pair for main part in the size to give the correct tension; one pair 4 sizes smaller for edgings

MAIN PIECE

Knit the following pieces from the charts, noting special instructions for smaller pieces which are worked as sections of the large diamonds, omitting the central motif.

Jacket	Coat
a = 17 pieces	a = 24 pieces
aa = 2 pieces	aa = 2 pieces
b1 = 1 piece	b1 = 2 pieces
b2 = 1 piece	b2 = 2 pieces
c1 = 3 pieces	c1 = 3 pieces
c2 = 2 pieces	c2 = 2 pieces
c3 = 1 piece	c3 = 1 piece
d = 1 piece	
e = 1 piece	
f = 1 piece	f = 1 piece
g = 1 piece	g = 1 piece

EDGINGS

Jacket: work as Tapestry Flower design, but using the smaller needles.

Coat: work in garter st, using the smaller needles and following the shaping as given for Tapestry Flower design.

FINISHING

Position pieces as in layout diagram, noting slight variations in direction of pieces aa and b, and taking care to position pieces b1, b2, c1, c2, and c3 correctly as shown, to maintain the continuity of leaf pattern. Complete finishing exactly as Tapestry Flower design, omitting embroidery.

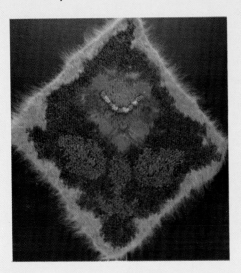

TAPESTRY FLOWER DESIGN

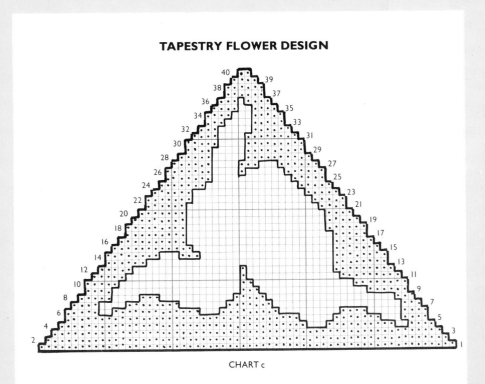

CHART c

SANDY BLACK

FLOWER TUNIC AND SWEATER

This design can be made as a longline tunic or sweater and is knitted in Rowan's Sandy Black Wool Twist in stocking stitch with 8 large stylised flower motifs placed over the body and sleeves. Two different motifs are illustrated, each worked from a chart, using 100% Angora to pick out part of the flower and create textural interest. The styling is very individual with the stand-up wrapover collar, tight sleeves and draped raglan shoulders plus edgings and collar worked in diagonal rib.

SIZES
There are two sizes to fit up to 36in/92cm or up to 40in/102cm bust.

TUNIC
Knitted measurements: length 34[35]in/ 86[89]cm; all round width at underarm 44[50]in/112[127]cm; sleeve length 28in/71cm.

SWEATER
Knitted measurements: length 24[25]in/ 61[64]cm; all round width at underarm 44[50]in/112[127]cm, sleeve length 28in/ 71cm.

ABBREVIATIONS
See page 15.

MATERIALS
TUNIC
○ 19[20] × 50g balls Rowan's Sandy Black Wool Twist in colours as follows:
    16[17] balls in main colour (MC)
    1 ball in each of 3 contrast colours (A, B, C)
○ 2 × 20g balls 100% Angora in each of 2 contrast colours (D and E)

SWEATER
○ 15[16] × 50g balls Rowan's Sandy Black Wool Twist in colours as follows:
    12[13] balls in main colour (MC)
    1 ball in each of 3 contrast colours (A, B, C)
○ 2 × 20g balls 100% Angora in each of 2 contrast colours (D and E)
○ 2 pairs of needles are required, one pair for main parts in the size to give the correct tension; one pair 3 sizes smaller for edgings

TENSION
Measured over st st, 18 sts and 24 rows to 4in/10cm using 5½mm (UK size 5) needles or the size to give correct tension. Recommended needles for edging: 4mm (UK size 8).
To avoid disappointment, it is essential to check your tension carefully before commencing the garment and use the needles which give **you** the correct tension. **This may not be the size quoted in the standard tension**, as individual knitters vary.

How to check tension: Using the recommended needes and MC, cast on 30 sts and work in stocking stitch for 36 rows. Cast off. Pin the square down flat without stretching. Place a pin between 2 sts near the left, count 18 sts and mark with another pin between the 18th and 19th sts. Measure out 24 rows in the same way. Measure the distance between pins. This should be 4in/10cm in both directions. If it is less your knitting is too tight – try one size larger needle. If it is more, your knitting is too loose – try one size smaller needle. Repeat the process until the correct tension is achieved. Do not be afraid to go up or down more than one needle size. Adjust the size of the second pair of needles accordingly.

NOTES ON WORKING PATTERN
Tunic and sweater are worked in st st with three lotus flower motifs on front and back, and one on each sleeve. These motifs are worked from a chart and placed according to instructions. One square of chart represents one stitch. Odd numbered rows (rs) are knit-read from right to left; even numbered rows (ws) are purl-read from left to right. Use a separate ball or length of yarn for each area of colour, and cross the yarns when changing colour to link the colours and prevent holes appearing in the knitting.

TUNIC
BACK
Using the smaller needles and MC, cast on

102 [114] sts and work diagonal rib as follows:

Row 1(rs): (k3, p3) rep to end.
Row 2(ws): (k2, p3, k1) rep to end.
Row 3: (p2, k3, p1) rep to end.
Row 4: (p3, k3) rep to end.
Row 5: (k1, p3, k2) rep to end.
Row 6: (p1, k3, p2) rep to end.
Work rows 1–6 once more.**
Change to the larger needles and beg with a k row, work in st st for 12 [14] rows.
Place first motif as follows:
Next row: k11 [17]MC, work 40 sts from row 1 of chart thus: k19MC, 2A, 19MC, k51 [57]MC.
Next row: p51 [57]MC, work 40 sts from row 2 of chart thus: p19MC, 2A, 19MC, p11 [17]MC.
Cont in this way, working each row of chart in turn until row 50 is complete.
Work in st st for 4 [6] rows.
Place second motif as follows (rs facing):
Next row: k51 [57]MC, work 40 sts from row 1 of chart thus; k19MC, 2A, 19MC, k11 [17]MC.
Next row: p11 [17]MC, work 40 sts from row 2 of chart thus: p19MC, 2A, 19MC, p51 [57]MC.
Cont in this way, rep each row of chart in turn until row 50 is complete.
Work in st st for 8 [10] rows.
Shape armholes and place third motif as follows:
Next row: cast off 3 [5] sts, k28 [32]MC, work 40 sts from row 1 of chart thus: k19MC, 2A, 19MC, k31 [37]MC.
Next row: cast off 3 [5] sts, p28 [32]MC, work 40 sts from row 2 of chart thus: p19MC, 2A, 19MC, p28 [32]MC. 96 [104] sts.
Cont to work each row of chart in turn, shape armholes as follows:
Work a further 4 rows in patt, then dec 1st at both ends of next and every foll 5th row until 82 [90] sts rem. Now dec 1st at both ends of every foll alt row until row 42 of chart is complete.
Cont in st st only, dec on every alt row as before until 58 [62] sts rem.
Now dec 1st at both ends of foll row until 44 [48] sts remain.
Cast off.

FRONT
Work as for Back until 62 [68] sts rem.
Shape front neck:
Next row: p22 [25], turn and leave rem sts on a spare needle.
Cont to dec at armhole edge as before, at the same time dec 1st at neck edge on every row until 4 [3] sts remain. Cast off.
With rs facing, return to sts on spare needle and cast off next 18 sts. Now complete to match first side of neck.

SWEATER
BACK
Work as for Tunic to **.

Change to the larger needles and beg with a k row work in st st for 10 [12] rows.
Place 2 motifs as follows:
Next row: k7 [13]MC, work 40 sts of row 1 from chart thus: k19MC, 2A, 19MC, k8MC, then work 40 sts of row 1 from chart as given, k7 [13]MC.
Next row: p7 [13]MC, work 40 sts of row 2 from chart thus: p19MC, 2A, 19MC, p8MC,

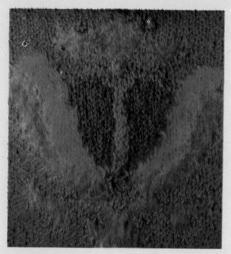 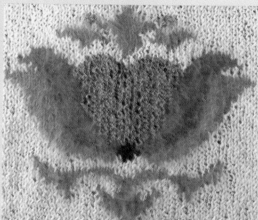

then work 40 sts of row 2 from chart as given, p7 [13]MC.
Cont in this way rep each row of chart in turn until row 50 is complete.
Proceed in st st only until work measures 12½ [13]in/32 [33]cm, ending with a ws row.
Shape armholes and place motif as for tunic.
Complete as for tunic.

FRONT
Work as for Back until 62 [68] sts rem.
Shape front neck as for tunic.

SLEEVES (Both Styles)
Using the smaller needles and MC cast on 30 sts and work 12 rows diagonal rib as for Back.
Change to the larger needles and beg with a k row work 10 rows st st.
Inc 1st at both ends of next and every foll 3rd row until there are 56 sts.
Now inc 1st at both ends of every foll alt row until there are 76 sts. Purl 1 row. Place markers at each end of row for armholes.
Cont with no further shaping place motif as follows:
Next row: k18MC, work 40 sts from row 1 of chart thus, k19MC, 2A, 19MC, k18MC.
Next row: p18MC, work 40 sts from row 2 of chart thus, p19MC, 2A, 19MC, p19MC.
Cont in this way until row 50 is complete.
Work 2 rows in st st.
Shape sleeve:
Next row: k38, turn, leave rem sts on a spare needle.
Dec 1st at beg of next and foll 6th row. Then dec 1st at centre edge on foll 3rd row. Now

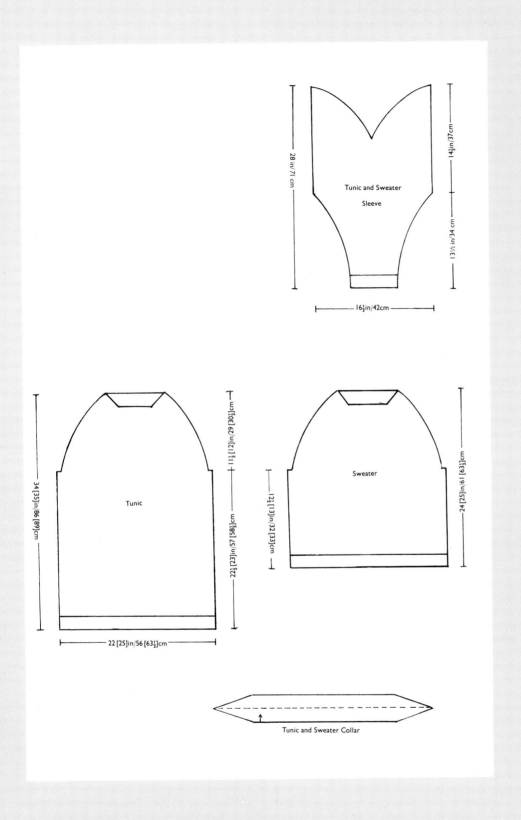

28 in/71 cm

14½in/37cm

Tunic and Sweater
Sleeve

13½ in/34 cm

16½in/42cm

34 [35]in/86 [89]cm

11½ [12]in/29 [30½]cm

Tunic

22½ [23]in/57 [58½]cm

22 [25]in/56 [63½]cm

Sweater

24 [25]in/61 [63½]cm

12½ [13]in/32 [33]cm

Tunic and Sweater Collar

dec Ist at same edge on every foll alt row until 28 sts rem. Dec Ist at same edge on every row until 19 sts rem. Cast off at same edge 4 sts at beg of next and foll alt row. Work 1 row. Place marker on centre edge before casting off rem 11 sts.

With rs of work facing rejoin yarn to sts on spare needle and work to match first side of sleeve.

COLLAR (Both styles)

Using the smaller needles and MC, cast on 108 sts and work in diagonal rib as for back, and at the same time cast on 3 sts at beg of every row until there are 162 sts incorporating the extra sts into patt. Work 2 rows straight then cast off 3 sts at beg of every row until there are 108 sts. Cast off.

FINISHING

Carefully darn in all loose ends, closing any gaps in the knitting and working up and down and not across wrong side of work.

Using backstitch, join centre sleeve seams. Join outer edges of sleeves between markers to raglan shapings of front and back, easing surplus of sleeves to top of armholes, giving fullness at shoulder. Join side and sleeve seams. Fold collar in half, cast on and cast off edges tog, and oversew tog. Working from the ws, oversew collar to neck edge, overlapping collar at front so points meet the shoulder seams.

TAPESTRY FLOWER VERSION

An equally attractive alternative to the Lotus Flower motif is the Tapestry Flower as used in the Patchwork Jacket and Coat. Simply substitute the 40 sts and 50 rows of the new chart in the Lotus Flower instructions — sweater or tunic style.

MATERIALS

○ 19 [20] or 15 [16] × 50g balls of Rowan's Sandy Black Wool Twist for tunic or sweater as follows:

   16 [17] or 12 [13] balls in main colour (MC)
   2 balls in first contrast (B) (leaf colour)
   1 ball each in 2nd and 3rd contrasts (C) and (D)

○ 1 × 20g ball of 100% Angora in each of 1st and 2nd flower colours (F) and (G)
○ oddments of 2 wool colours for embroidery

Colourways illustrated:

a) MC = Stone, B = Eau de nil, C = Mid-Grey, D = Rose, F = Cedar, G = Grape.

b) MC = Red, B = Emerald, C = Purple, D = Claret, F = Bright Blue, G = Fuchsia.

Work tunic or sweater exactly as Lotus Flower design, except that first 2 rows of chart are as follows:

Chart row 1: knit 17MC, 2B, 2MC, 2B, 17MC.

Chart row 2: purl 15MC, 10B, 15MC. Cont working from Tapestry Flower chart.

Embroidery: using the 2 oddment colours

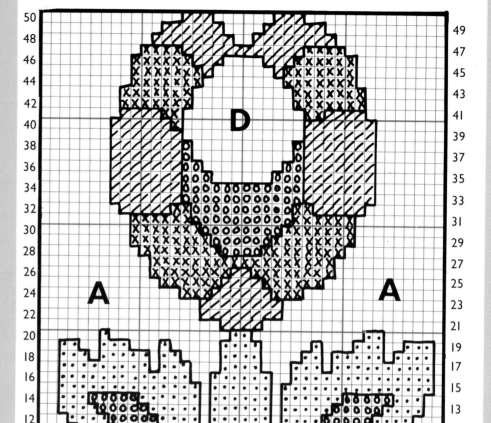

TAPESTRY FLOWER

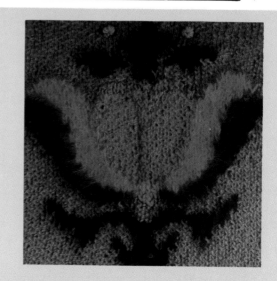

LOTUS FLOWER

alternately, work a curved line of French knots on each flower along the line between the upper and lower halves of centre.

Lotus Flower

□ = MC		
· = A		
⊠ = B	wool colours	
◪ = C		
⧄ = D	angora colours	
⊙ = E		

Tapestry Flower

□ = A or D		
· = B	wool colours	
⊙ = C		
⊠ = F	angora colours	
⧄ = G		

ROSETTE

This generously sized sweater is knitted in stocking stitch in a combination of 2 yarns, one plain and one textured. The design of small circles forming 'rosettes' of colours can be made in either luxurious 100% angora or 100% cotton chenille, on a background of Wool Twist or Aran Tweed for a slightly heavier garment. Best combinations are Tweed with Chenille and Wool Twist with Angora.

SIZE

One size to fit up to 40in/102cm bust.
Knitted measurements: width at underarm 22in/56cm; length 27in/68½cm; sleeve length 27in/68½cm.

ABBREVIATIONS

See page 15.

MATERIALS

○ 550g Rowan Wool Twist or 600g Rowanspun Tweed in main colour (MC)
○ I ball each of Wool Twist in 3 contrast colours for centres of circles
○ Plus either:
16 × 20g balls 100% Angora in 4 colours as follows:
  7 balls in first contrast colour
  3 balls each in 2nd, 3rd and 4th contrast colours
or:
6 × 50g balls of Rowan Fine Cotton Chenille, as follows:
  3 balls in first contrast colour
  I ball each in 2nd, 3rd and 4th contrast colours
○ 2 pairs of needles are required, one pair for main parts in size to give correct tension; one pair 3 sizes smaller for edgings
○ I large-eyed yarn needle
○ I stitch holder

TENSION

20 sts and 21 rows to 4in/10cm, measured over pattern using 5½mm (UK size 5) needles or the size to give correct tension. Recommended needles for edgings: 4mm (UK size 8).
To avoid disappointment, it is essential to check tension carefully before commencing the garment and use the needles which give **you** the correct tension. **This may not be the size quoted in the standard tension**, as individual knitters vary.
How to check tension: Read paragraph Notes on working pattern. Using the recommended needles and MC, cast on 28 sts and joining in colours as required, work a section from chart for back as follows: starting from row I with a knit row, work from sts I to 28 on knit rows and 28 to I on purl rows, until row 28 is complete. Cast off loosely. Pin the square down flat without

stretching. Place a pin between 2 sts near the left, count 20 sts and mark with another pin between the 20th and 21st sts. Mark out 21 rows in the same way. Measure the distance between the pins. This should be 4in/10cm in both directions. If it is less, your knitting is too tight – try one size larger size needle. If it is more, your knitting is too loose – try one size smaller needle. Repeat the process until the correct tension is achieved. Do **not** be afraid to go up or down more than one needle size. Adjust the needle size for edgings accordingly.

NOTES ON WORKING PATTERN

One square of chart represents one stitch. Odd numbered rows (rs) are knit – read from right to left; even numbered rows (ws) are purl – read from left to right. Use I ball of background wool across each row, but use separate balls of contrast yarn for each coloured rosette of 7 circles and also for the circles in first contrast between rosettes. Do not strand background wool across more than 4 sts and do not strand contrast yarn between the rosettes. Cross yarns where they meet to prevent gaps appearing in the knitting. Take care not to pull the colours at the back too tight or this will distort the knitting. To minimize tangling, wind bobbins (made from card) of contrast yarns, and allow these to hang close to the needle, unravelling a short amount at a time as required.
Embroidery: the three extra Wool Twist colours are used to fill in the centres of the 7 circles which form each coloured rosette, using 'Swiss darning' technique. After knitting is completed and before making up, cover the centres of all the rosette circles with one of the 3 contrast colours, used at random within each rosette (see diagram). Alternatively, expert knitters may prefer to substitute these colours for background yarn when actually knitting the rosettes.

BACK

Using the smaller needles and MC, cast on 108 sts and work edging as follows in diagonal rib:
Row I: (k3, p3) to end.
Row 3: (k2, p3, kI) to end.
Row 3: (p2, k3, pI) to end.
Row 4: (p3, k3) to end.
Row 5: (kI, p3, k2) to end.
Row 6: (pI, k3, p2) to end.
Work rows I – 6 twice more or until edging measures 2in/5cm, inc I st at beg and end of last row. 110 sts. Change to the larger needles and beg working from chart for back at row I with a knit row. Join in angora or chenille as required and work straight until row 76 is complete.
Shape raglan: cast off 3 sts at beg of next 2 rows. Work I row. Dec I st at each end of next and every foll alt row until row 124 is

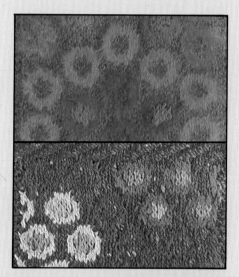

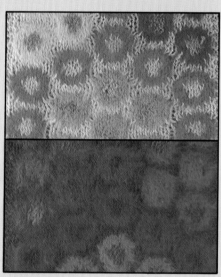

complete. 58 sts.* Dec I st at each end of next and every row until chart is complete. 42 sts. Cast off loosely.

FRONT

Work as for back to *.
Divide for neck:
Row 125: k2tog, patt 14 sts, turn and leave rem sts on st holder. Cont in patt on these 15 sts, dec I st at each end of every row until I st rem. Fasten off. Place sts from st holder back onto needles. With rs facing, rejoin yarn, cast off next 26 sts for centre front, patt to last 2 sts, k2tog, 15 sts. Working on these sts, dec I st at each end of every row to I st. Fasten off.

To Swiss darn centre of circles: For ease and speed of working Swiss darn the entire centre as 1 row of 4 long sts as shown. The centre 2 sts cover 4 knitted rows, the outer 2 sts cover 2 knitted rows.

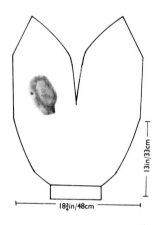

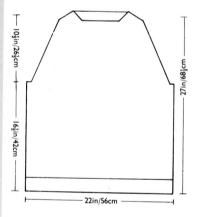

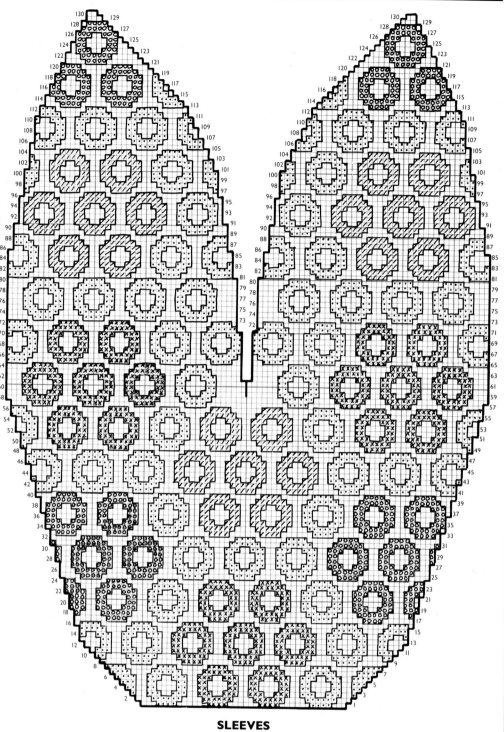

SLEEVES

SLEEVES

Using the smaller needles and MC, cast on 36 sts and work edging as for back, inc 4 sts evenly across last row. 40 sts. Change to the larger needles and beg working from chart for sleeve at row 1 with a knit row, shaping as follows:

Inc 1 st at each end of every foll row until row 13 is complete. Work 2 rows straight. Inc 1 st at each end of next and every foll 3rd row until row 58 is complete. 94 sts.

Divide for centre seam:

Next row, row 59: Patt 47, turn and leave rem sts on st holder. Work 2 rows. Dec 1 st at centre edge of next and every foll 10th row until row 81 is complete. Work 4 rows straight. Dec 1 st at each end of next and every foll 5th row until row 101 is complete.

Work 1 row. Dec 1 st at centre edge of next and every foll alt row and **at the same time** cont dec 1 st at side edge of every 5th row until row 111 is complete. Work 1 row. Dec 1 st at each end of next row. Dec 1 st at centre edge of next and every foll row and **at the same time** dec 1 st at side edge of next and every foll alt row until 2 sts rem. Fasten off. With rs facing, replace 47 sts from st holder onto needles, rejoin yarn and complete to match first side, reversing shapings.

COLLAR

Using the smaller needles and MC, cast on 132 sts and work collar in diagonal rib as for back. Work straight until collar measures 5½in/14cm. Cast off loosely in rib.

FINISHING

Darn in all loose ends carefully, closing up gaps at the same time.

Angora version: do not press.

Chenille version: using a damp cloth, lightly steam press pieces, avoiding edgings.

Both versions:

Embroidery (if applicable): using Swiss darning technique, cover centre of all circles forming rosettes with one of the 3 additional contrast colours, see diagram. Using backstitch, join centre sleeve seams then raglan seams. Join side and sleeve seams. Using a flat oversewn seam, and working from ws, join collar to neck edge, with the opening at centre front.

Angora – colourways illustrated

- ⊠ = teal blue or teal blue ⎤
- ⧄ = burgundy or navy ⎥
- · = khaki or fuchsia ⎥ *angora colours*
- ⊙ = grape or burgundy ⎦
- MC ☐ = slate grey or purple ⎤ *wool*

Chenille version

- ⊠ = turquoise green ⎤
- ⧄ = carnation pink ⎥
- · = purple [1st contrast] ⎥ *chenille*
- ⊙ = steel blue ⎦
- MC ☐ = fig ⎤ *wool tweed*

BACK AND FRONT

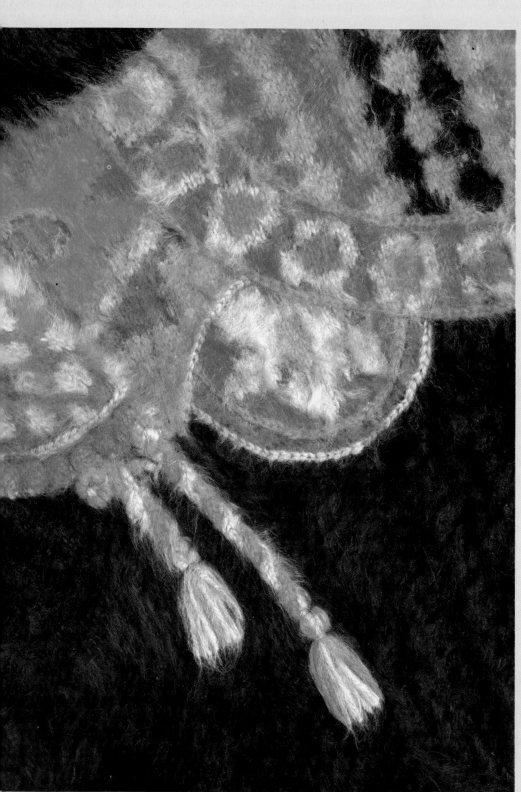

MERRYGOROUND

The main body of this luxurious wraparound coat is worked in a textured cable twist stitch, which is used to create the twisted braid effect. The patterned sections over the shoulders are worked from charts in a combination of fairisle and block knitting, and embellished with embroidery and tassels to complete the ornate detailing.

SIZE
One size to fit up to 38in/97cm bust.
Knitted measurements: back width at underarm 24in/61cm; length 36in/91½cm inc edging; sleeve length 24in/61cm.

ABBREVIATIONS
See page 15.

MATERIALS
○ 48 × 20g balls of 100% Angora or 48 × 25g balls of Mohair in 6 colours as follows:
　　36 balls in main colour (MC), Grey or Black
　　2 balls each in Bright Blue (Bl), Emerald (E) and Burgundy (Bg)
　　3 balls each in Red (R) and Khaki (K)
○ I pair of needles is required in the size to give the correct tension
○ cable needle
○ pair of shoulder pads
○ large eyed yarn needle

TENSION
Measured over fairisle diamond pattern, 20 sts and 20 rows to 4in/10cm using 5½mm (UK size 5) needles.
To avoid disappointment it is essential to check your tension carefully before starting the garment and use needles which give **you** the correct tension. **This may not be the size quoted in the standard tension**, as individual knitters vary.
How to check tension: Using the recommended needles and Bg, cast on 25 sts, join in K, and work in fairisle as follows:
Row I: knit IBg, (3Bg, IK, 4Bg) 3 times.
Row 2: purl IBg, (2Bg, 3K, 3Bg) 3 times.
Row 3: knit IBg, (IBg, 5K, 2Bg) 3 times.
Row 4: purl IBg, (7K, IBg) 3 times.
Row 5: knit IBg, (IBg, 5K, 2Bg) 3 times.
Row 6: purl IBg, (2Bg, 3K, 3Bg) 3 times.
Rep rows 1–6 4 times more.
Cast off loosely. Pin the piece down flat without stretching. Place a pin between 2 sts near the left, count 20 sts, and mark with another pin between the 20th and 21st sts. Mark out 20 rows in the same way. Measure the distance between pins. This should be 4in/10cm in both directions. If it is less your knitting is too tight – try one size larger needle. If it is more, your knitting is too loose – try one size smaller needle. Repeat the process until the correct tension is achieved.

Do not be afraid to go up or down more than one needle size.

NOTES ON WORKING PATTERN

One square of chart represents one stitch. Odd numbered rows (rs) are knit – read from right to left; even numbered rows (ws) are purl – read from left to right. Some areas (e.g. crosses) are worked in fairisle – strand colour not in use loosely at the back over not more than 3 sts. Larger areas of colour (e.g. flowers) are worked with separate balls of yarn. Cross yarns when changing colour to link the colours and prevent holes appearing in the knitting.

Coloured cables: where indicated, change to working 2 red, 2 khaki sts instead of 4 MC sts and strand MC behind contrast colours. When the 4 sts are cabled, maintain the continuity of the colours so they twist around each other. All coloured cables are worked in red and khaki throughout.

Bobbles: where ◪, ■ or ◩ is marked on the chart work a bobble on this st as follows, using the contrast colour indicated:
On knit rows: k into front, back and front of this st, turn and k3, turn and p3. Pass the 2nd and 3rd sts over the first and cont in background colour. When bobbles occur on purl rows, work as above, but push bobble through to rs when complete.

BACK

Using MC cast on 88 sts and work as follows:
Row 1 (rs): knit.
Row 2 (ws): purl.
Row 3: k2, (c4b, k4) 10 times, c4b, k2.
Row 4: purl.
Row 5: knit.
Row 6: purl, inc 1 st at beg and end of row.
Row 7: k3, (c4b, k4) 10 times, c4b, k3.
Cont in cable patt as set, working a cable every 4th row and inc 1 st at each end of row 12 and every foll 6th row. Incorporate extra sts into cable patt as they occur.
When work measures 6in/15cm and a ws row is complete, change the 9th cable from right edge to a 2-colour cable, using khaki and red. Cont in cable patt, inc as before until work measures 9in/23cm, ending with a ws row. Change the cable to the right of the first coloured cable into a 2-colour cable, using khaki and red. Cont in cable patt as now set, still inc every 6th row until there are 116 sts and work measures 17in/43cm, ending with a ws row. Start working patt from chart A at row 1, gradually introducing cols as required and fading cable patt into colour patterns. Use separate balls of MC each side of patt. Work until row 26 is complete. 120 sts.
Shape armholes: keeping continuity of patt cast off 6 sts at beg of next 2 rows, and 3 sts at beg of foll 2 rows. Cast off 2 sts at beg of next 2 rows. Dec 1 st at beg of next 10 rows. 88 sts. Work straight from chart until row 76 is complete.

Shape shoulders: cast off 6 sts at beg of next 4 rows. Cast off 7 sts at beg of next 4 rows. Cast off rem 36 sts loosely.

RIGHT FRONT

Using MC, cast on 26 sts, knit 1 row, purl 1 row.
Row 3(rs): cast on 5 sts, k9, (c4b, k4) twice, c4b, k2.
Row 4(ws): purl.
Row 5: cast on 4 sts, knit to last st, inc 1.
Row 6: purl, inc in last st.
Row 7: inc in first st, k5, (c4b, k4) 3 times, c4b, k3.
* Cont in cable patt as set, shaping side edge by inc 1 st on row 12 and every foll 6th row as back. **At the same time** shape curved front edge as follows:
Inc 1 st on next and foll 4 rows.
Inc 1 st on foll 8 alt rows.
Inc 1 st on every foll 3rd row, 6 times. 63 sts.
Cont straight at front edge, but still inc at side edge every 6th row until work measures 10in/25½cm, ending with a ws row.
Convert the first cable at front edge into a 2-colour cable and cont (still shaping side edge as before) until work measures 17in/43cm ending with a ws row. Change the 5th cable from front edge into a 2 colour cable and cont in cable patt as now set, still inc at side edge until there are 72 sts. Work straight until front measures 19½in/49½cm. Start working colour pattern from chart B, shaping front neck edge from row 4 by dec 1 st on every alt row, and beg armhole shaping on row 14 and shoulder shaping on row 64 to correspond with back.

LEFT FRONT

Using MC cast on 26 sts and k 1 row.
Row 2(ws): cast on 5 sts, p to end.
Row 3(rs): k2, (c4b, k4) 3 times, k5.
Row 4: cast on 4 sts, p to end.
Row 5: k to end.
Row 6: inc in first st, p to last st, inc in last st.
Row 7: k3, (c4b, k4) 4 times, k1, inc in last st.
Cont as for right front from * but introducing 2 coloured cables as follows: start first coloured cable after 7½in/19cm on the 5th cable from front edge. Start second coloured cable after 11in/28cm on the 6th cable from front edge. When work measures 15in/38cm beg working from chart C at row 1. Complete front from chart, shaping as shown.

RIGHT SLEEVE

Using MC, cast on 50sts and beg cable patt as follows:
Row 1: knit.
Row 2: purl.
Row 3: k3, (k4, c4b) 5 times, k7.
Cont in cable patt, cabling every 4th row and shaping sleeve by inc 1 st at each end of next and every 4th row, incorporating extra sts into patt * until there are 80 sts, and work measures 12½in/32cm, ending with a ws row. Beg working from chart D at row 1 with a k row, inc as before on every 4th row until there are 90 sts. Cont until row 22 is complete.

Shape top: cast off 3 sts at beg of next 4 rows. Cast off 2 sts at beg of next 2 rows. Work 1 row.
Dec 1 st at each end of next and foll 8 alt rows. Dec 1 st at each end of next 6 rows. Cast off 3

CHART A: BACK

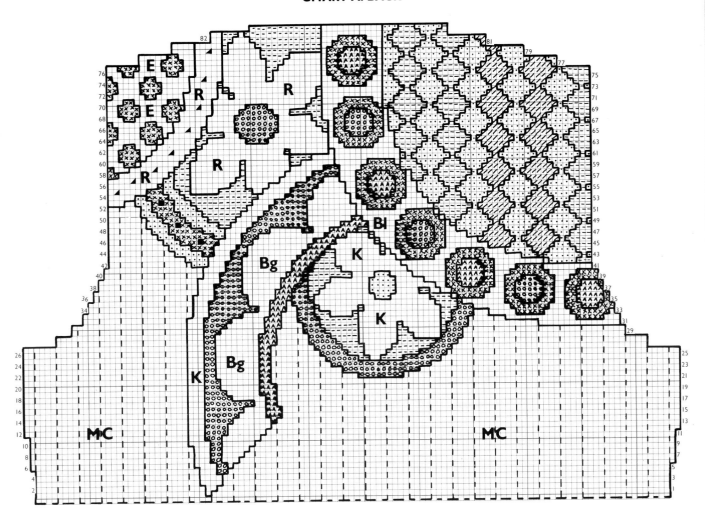

sts at beg of next 2 rows. Cast off 4 sts at beg of next 2 rows. Cast off 5 sts at beg of next 2 rows. Cast off rem 20 sts.

LEFT SLEEVE

Work as for right sleeve to * and cont shaping until there are 90 sts and sleeve measures 17in/43cm. At the same time introduce 3-coloured cables as follows on rs rows: after 10in/25cm and a ws row is complete, change central cable into a 2-colour cable. After 13in/33cm, change the cable to the left of the central one to a 2-colour cable. After 14in/35cm, change the cable to the right of the central one to a 2-colour cable. Cont in this way until sleeve measures 17in/43cm.
Shape top: shape as given for right sleeve but following chart E, and fading cables (including coloured ones) into patt.

COLLAR AND EDGING

With MC, cast on 29 sts and knit 1 row. Beg patt as follows:

Row 1(rs): p1, (sl 3, p1) rep to end.
Row 2(ws): knit.
Row 3: purl.
Row 4: knit.
Row 5: purl.
Row 6: k2, (k next st tog with strand of yarn below on p side, k3) rep to end, ending last rep k2.
Row 7: p3, (sl 3, p1) rep to last 2 sts, p2.
Rows 8 to 11: as rows 2 to 5.
Row 12: k4, (k next st tog with strand of yarn below on p side, k3) rep to end, ending last rep k4.
These 12 rows form patt. Cont until work measures 30in/76cm.
Shape collar: keeping continuity of patt, inc 1 st at each end of the next and every foll 6th row until there are 57 sts. Work straight until edging measures 53in/134½cm from beg. Dec 1 st at each end of next and every foll 6th row until 29 sts remain. Cont straight for a further 50in/127cm. Leave sts on a thread.

FINISHING AND EMBROIDERY

Do not press. Darn in loose ends carefully on inside of work, closing any gaps. Join shoulder seams and set in sleeves. Work chain stitch outlines in red or khaki as appropriate around curved lines of pattern. Embroider flowers at tops of coloured cables as follows: using yarn double, in blue, red, or khaki, work straight sts to form 5 or 6 petals with a contrast centre. Make tassels in red and khaki and secure to base of each coloured cable.
Join side and sleeve seams. Turn up ¾in/2cm at cuff to inside and slipstitch in place. With rs together, place centre of collar to centre back, and pin edging all round front and lower edges, easing around front curves, until the two ends meet at the side seam. Adjust length if necessary by unravelling or knitting extra length in patt. Cast off. Backstitch edging in position, join edging seam, turn to inside and slipstitch neatly in place. Insert shoulder pads. To complete the coat, make a silk lining – see p. 12.

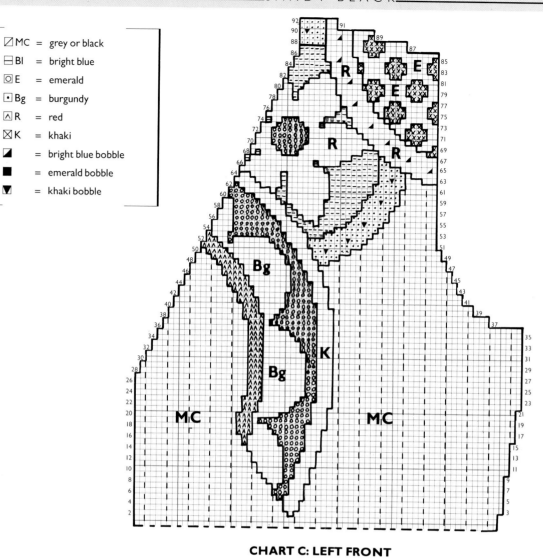

	MC	=	grey or black
	Bl	=	bright blue
	E	=	emerald
	Bg	=	burgundy
	R	=	red
	K	=	khaki
		=	bright blue bobble
		=	emerald bobble
		=	khaki bobble

CHART C: LEFT FRONT

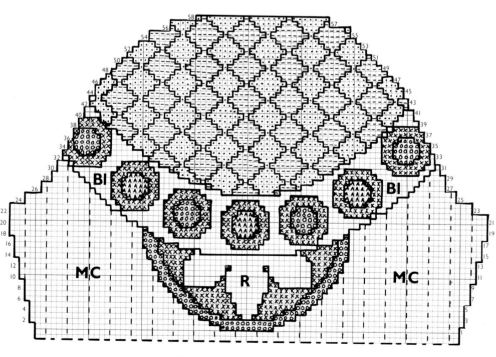

CHART D: RIGHT SLEEVE

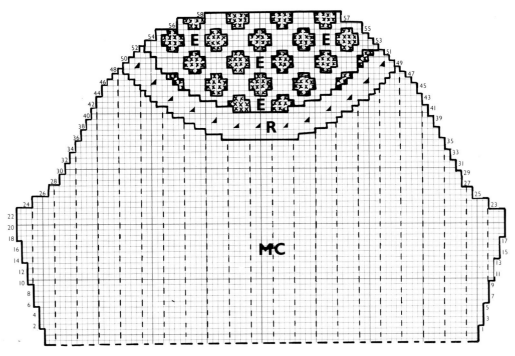

CHART E: LEFT SLEEVE

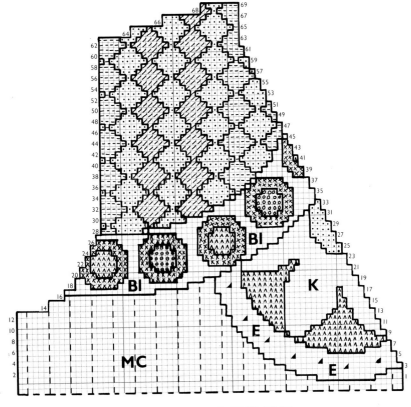

CHART B: RIGHT FRONT

YARNS AND TENSIONS INDEX

Designs knitted in Mohair

Bobbly Grid cardigan; Dogtooth Check jacket and sweater; Curves cardigan; Fairisle Fun sweater; Triangles sweater; Fans cardigan; Rectangles sweater; Rose jacket; Iris cardigan; Trailing Roses sweater; Textured Tartan sweater (combined with cotton).

The mohair yarn has a minimum 75% mohair content, with a wool/nylon binder.

Length: 49metres/53yards per 25g ball.

Recommended tension over stocking stitch: 16 sts and 20 rows to 4in/10cm using 5½mm (UK size 5) needles, which is a fairly loose and open tension to bring out the best in such a beautiful fibre. (Please refer to Tension section on p11.)

All mohair designs are available in kit form by mail order from Sandy Black, see below for details. The particular colours used in the designs are also available in Spunlaine Mohair, obtainable from stockists or by mail order from Sandy Black (see below).

Designs knitted in 100% Angora

Curves cardigan; Iris cardigan; Iris or Plain batwing sweater; Trailing Roses jacket; Merrygoround coat; Vase of Flowers coat.

This yarn is wonderfully soft and the ultimate in luxury, better than any fur!

Length: 50metres/54yards per 20g ball.

Recommended tensions over stocking stitch: 18 sts and 22 rows to 4in/10cm using 5½mm (UK size 5) needles; or 16 sts and 20 rows using 6mm (UK size 4) needles, but please refer to tension paragraph.

Yarn and kits for all designs available by mail order from Sandy Black.

Designs knitted in Sandy Black Wool Twist (100% wool) by Rowan Yarns

Lion and Unicorn sweater* and cardigan; Shield sweater* and cardigan; Fleur de Lys sweater*; Small Shields sweater*; Stained Glass sweater.

This yarn gives an attractive crinkly texture to your knitting, which enhances even the simplest stitches.

Length: 95metres/105yards per 50g ball.

Recommended tension over stocking stitch: 18 sts and 24 rows to 4in/10cm using 5½mm (UK size 5) needles, but please refer to tension paragraph.

Wool Twist with 100% Angora

Patchwork Flower coat and jacket; Flower tunic and sweater (2 versions); Rosette sweater.

Wool Twist with Rowan Fine Cotton Chenille

Patchwork Leaf jacket; Rosette sweater (version).

For tension, **see** Wool Twist.

All Wool Twist designs are available as kits by mail order from Sandy Black; selected designs (marked *) available as kits from Rowan stockists (see below).

Designs knitted in Salad Days 100% Cotton by Rowan Yarns

Fairisle Fun cardigan; Matisse dress; Posy Trellis cardigan*; Textured Tartan sweater (with mohair).

This textured cotton gives an interesting surface to stocking stitch designs, and combines well with mohair.

Length: 180metres/195yards per 50g ball.

Recommended tension over stocking stitch: 22 sts and 27 rows to 4in/10cm using 4mm (UK size 8) needles, but please refer to tension paragraph.

Yarn and kits available from Rowan stockists or by mail order from Sandy Black.

YARN SUPPLIERS

Mail Order

All designs and yarns in the book – Mohair, 100% Angora, Wool Twist and Cotton – are available by mail order in kit form from:
Sandy Black, Dept K, 54–58 Tanner Street, London SE1.

Please write for details of prices and yarn samples for all kits, enclosing a stamped addressed envelope. (Export service available for individual orders.)

Stockists

Rowan Yarns and Sandy Black Kits by Rowan (designs marked *) are available from Rowan stockists, including:

London (central): Ries Wools, 242 High Holborn, WC1; Liberty, Regent St, W1; John Lewis, Oxford St, W1; Creativity, 45 New Oxford St, WC1; Colourway, 112A Westbourne Grove, W2.

Edinburgh: Victoria Street Designs, 16 Victoria St.

Manchester: Couture Yarns, Royal Exchange Shopping Centre.

Holmfirth, Yorkshire: Upcountry, 12 Towngate.

Skipton, Yorkshire: Cloud Nine, 15 Sheep St.

Brighton: Ritzyknits, 37 Bond St.

Cardiff: Siop Jen, 36–38 Castle Arcade.

For full list of stockists, please write to: Rowan Yarns, Dept SB, Green Lane Mill, Holmfirth, HD7 1RW, W. Yorkshire, England. Tel: 0484 687374/686714.

Mohair yarns: All the above stockists carry a good selection of mohair yarns, but in case of difficulty, contact Ries Wools, 242 High Holborn, London WC1. Tel: 01-242 7721.
For stockists of Spunlaine Mohair please write to: Spunlaine Wools, Dept SB, Hanover Street Mills, Keighley, BD21 3QJ, W. Yorkshire, England. Tel: 0535 600803.

Overseas Distributors for Rowan Yarns United States: Westminster Trading Corporation, 5 Northern Boulevard, Amherst, New Hampshire 03031. Tel: 603-886 5041.
Australia: Sunspun Enterprises Pty, 195 Canterbury Rd, Canterbury 3126. Tel: 03-830 1609.
Canada: Estelle, 38 Continental Place, Scarborough, Ontario M1R 2T4. Please write for further information.
Melbourne, Australia: Mohair and 100% Angora yarns available from: Royal Arcade Knitting Centre, 6 Royal Arcade, Melbourne 3000. Tel 63 8555.

Beware! If you do not use the recommended yarns, successful results cannot be guaranteed. Good results can only be obtained if the tension matches those given above, and the length per ball also corresponds.

CARING FOR YOUR KNITTING

Hand Washing: I recommend **cold** water hand washing **only** for all the yarns in the book using a branded liquid detergent (eg Woolite) especially intended for a cold water wash. This avoids any problems with felting due to the wrong temperature water. When washing, squeeze your knitting, do not rub. Rinse thoroughly in cold water, give a short spin or roll garment in a towel to absorb excess water, then reshape and spread out flat to dry (preferably on a sweater dryer which allows the air to pass through). Keep away from direct sun and heat. Do not hang knitted garments even when dry, fold and keep flat. **Never** tumble dry knitwear, as this also creates felting.

Dry cleaning: the Wool Twist, Mohair and Cotton yarns can be successfully dry cleaned in general solvents; however, great caution must be exercised with the 100% Angora yarn. If not hand washing, then dry clean **only** by specialists who can use appropriate solvents (usually marked F), and not 'high street' dry cleaners. If the wrong solvents are used, disastrous shrinking will occur! For addresses of specialists please contact The Dry Cleaning Information Bureau. Tel: 01-863 8658.